STANFORD WHITE LETTERS TO HIS FAMILY

Laon Cathedral

STANFORD WHITE

LETTERS TO HIS FAMILY

Including a Selection of Letters to Augustus Saint-Gaudens

EDITED BY CLAIRE NICOLAS WHITE

RIZZOLI
NEW YORK

First published in the United States of America in 1997 by
Rizzoli International Publications, Inc.
300 Park Avenue South
New York, NY 10010

Library of Congress Cataloging-in-Publication Date
White, Stanford, 1853–1906
   Stanford White : letters to his family / edited by Claire Nicolas
White.
      p. cm.
   ISBN 0-8478-2022-X (hardcover)
   1. White, Stanford, 1853–1906--Correspondence. 2. Architects--
United States--Correspondence. 3. White, Stanford, 1853–1906--
Family. I. White, Claire Nicolas. 1929–   . II. Title.
NA737. W5A3   1997
720 .92--dc21
[B]   96-37364
                                                          CIP

Photographs of letters and drawings from the White family archive
© Zindman/Fremont

Designed by Tsang Seymour Design, New York

Printed in Singapore

CONTENTS

To the Memory of
Lawrence Grant White

NOTE

Stanford White was notorious for his idiosyncratic spelling and poor penmanship. In transcribing the correspondence, we have retained his original spelling without comment. As indicated, many of the letters are signed with his monogram, an S and W intertwined, or with a caricature of himself, often a profile with a jutting beard and a bristling head of hair.

ACKNOWLEDGMENTS

I wish to thank Mary Kaplan and the trustees of the Saint-Gaudens Memorial for their interest and sponsorship of this book. I also want to acknowledge Corona Machemer, who found the letters to Saint-Gaudens in *Architectural Record*, and Robert Hartman and James Lecky, who helped me organize the material. I am most grateful to Elizabeth Jones White who so ably finalized the project at Rizzoli.

Hudson Valley farm

INTRODUCTION

These letters and sketches by Stanford White were left to my husband by his father, Lawrence Grant White, when he died in 1956. He had mounted them in beautiful leather-bound books, each impetuously scribbled letter accompanied by a typewritten transcription. It was so obviously the labor of love and admiration of a son for his father that this alone made them precious.

Stanford White writes to the people closest to him—his parents, his wife, his son, and his great friend, the sculptor Augustus Saint-Gaudens. The letters very nearly span his lifetime, beginning with those written when he was a child and concluding with a letter to Saint-Gaudens written only a month before his death.

Stanford White was born in 1853. His relationship with his mother seems, from these letters, to have been remarkably affectionate, informal, and uninhibited in that era of Victorian formality. Alexina Mease White was a Southerner from Charleston and had written a book of children's verse.

Her husband, Richard Grant White, must have been more forbidding. An intellectual Anglophile, he felt frustrated all his life by his financially straitened circumstances. In spite of his reputation as a music critic and Shakespeare scholar, he was unable to pay for a college education for his sons. Instead, at the suggestion of Frederick Law Olmsted, a friend of his father's, Stanford was apprenticed to the eminent architect Henry Hobson Richardson. The painter John La Farge had been consulted about a possible painter's career, for which Stanford was definitely gifted, but he advised the young man that he would not be able to support himself. As to the older son, Richard Mansfield White, called Dick by his family, he actually went out West to dig for gold, with disappointing results.

When Stanford White came of age, his family lived at 118 East Tenth Street in New York, and the household also included Alexina's brother Charles Graham Mease and Richard Grant White's sister Gussie.

There must, then, have been a lot of

Hunter Mountain, New York

Smuggler's Notch, Mt. Mansfield, Vermont

pressure on Stanford White as a young man to make a fortune. His is a story of the Gilded Age: the meteoric rise to fame and success, and the tragic consquences—financial ruin and a violent death in 1906.

His overwhelming presence as a public figure, coupled with the painful trauma of his murder, made him a remote and secret shadow in the background of the family. It was a tragedy that my father-in-law kept very much to himself. Only at the end of these albums did he express his rage at his father's brutal death, writing after the last letter, "On the night of June 25th, 1906, while attending a performance at Madison Square Garden, Stanford White was shot from behind by a crazed profligate whose great wealth was used to besmirch his victim's memory during the series of notorious trials that ensued."

Whereas Stanford had been a reckless extrovert, Lawrence remained cautious and private. When he lost his father he was only seventeen. In 1956, when the movie *The Girl in the Red Velvet Swing* made the cover

of *Life* magazine, that issue did not enter the house and a nervousness set in that even I was aware of. Shortly thereafter Larry, as his friends called him, died suddenly of a heart attack.

He was an elegant man, with a hearty laugh and great warmth, though somewhat reserved. Passionately attached to Box Hill, the house that remained filled with treasures accumulated by his father, he mended its carpets and china and gardened tirelessly on weekends home from the office of McKim, Mead & White. How often we saw him sitting on the driveway pulling weeds or clipping the long rhododendron-lined drive, keeping the wilderness at bay. He accompanied his daughters singing at the piano, played four- and eight-hands with gusto, organized neighbors and some of his children into an orchestra, and painted watercolors. His distinguished translation of Dante's *Divine Comedy*, which he had begun for his own pleasure in about 1909, was published by Pantheon in 1948.

As a young married woman, I occasionally

Alexina Mease White by Daniel Huntington

Richard Grant White by Daniel Huntington

stayed in Box Hill to "keep house" for my father-in-law. I often felt intimidated by its standards, its grandeur, but a benign, unseen presence came to my rescue and reassured me. The more I found out about Stanford White, the more certain I was that it was he. And yet it took me years to piece together the story of what had happened.

It was Bessie Smith White, by then a splendid widow in her nineties, who first told me anecdotes about her husband, whom she reverently called Stanford White. Her stories were lighthearted, somewhat in awe. She described how she had longed to touch the top of his red hair when she first

spied him through the keyhole in her father's house; how he had bought her on the spot the huge terracotta pots she admired in Sicily, how he had urged her to throw handfuls of stones against the wet concrete walls of Box Hill as it was being built. When I married her grandson, Bessie gave us a modest sum of money to go on a honeymoon. "I know what a difference it makes!" she sighed.

I never noticed any bitterness in her. She was a very down-to-earth country woman who preferred simple pleasures such as fishing, boating, and croquet. Even though, at the end of her life, she spent the winter

Hunter Mountain, New York

Valley in the Catskills, New York

INTRODUCTION

months in New York, I doubt that she enjoyed the more formal life among the "high cockalorums" as Stanford himself called them with some irony.

Laura Chanler White, my mother-in-law, described Stanford White as one of the three men she had delighted in the most as a young girl, the two others being her own father, Winthrop Chanler, and Theodore Roosevelt. White was a close friend of the Chanlers and must have been fond of the spirited young Laura, who had ambitions of becoming a painter. He organized a party for her and her friends in the Madison Square Garden Tower, with her parents' approval. This suggests that his quarters there were more wholesome than is often reported. In June 1906 Laura spent a weekend in St. James with the Whites. At dinner on Sunday she sat next to Stanford. The next morning when the young people got up he had already left for his office in town. That same evening he was killed.

There is a curious vacuum on the White side of the family tree. Alexina Mease White had moved in with Stanford and Bessie after her husband's death in 1885. She continued to live with her daughter-in-law at Box Hill until she died in 1920. Richard Mansfield White was last seen at his brother's funeral, when he told the press that he had a family of his own in the West. There is a mystery about him that still intrigues me.

When I began reading these letters, a personality so delightful, so warm, mischievous, and alive emerged that I fell in love with this man I had never known.

That he was also an unusually sensitive, delicate artist is only too evident from these watercolors painted in his youth and the quick architectural notations made during his study trip in France. To give some idea of the enormous amount of work he accomplished as an architect and designer during his relatively short life, I have included, besides the personal letters to his family as collected by his son, a group of letters to Saint-Gaudens. Published in 1911 in *Architectural Record*, they evoke the kind of painstaking collaboration between artist and architect that has largely disappeared in our time. They also show, as Saint-Gaudens put it, "an almost feminine tenderness to his friends," as well as a generous spirit and, of course, an unfailing aesthetic judgment.

CLAIRE NICOLAS WHITE
ST. JAMES, NEW YORK

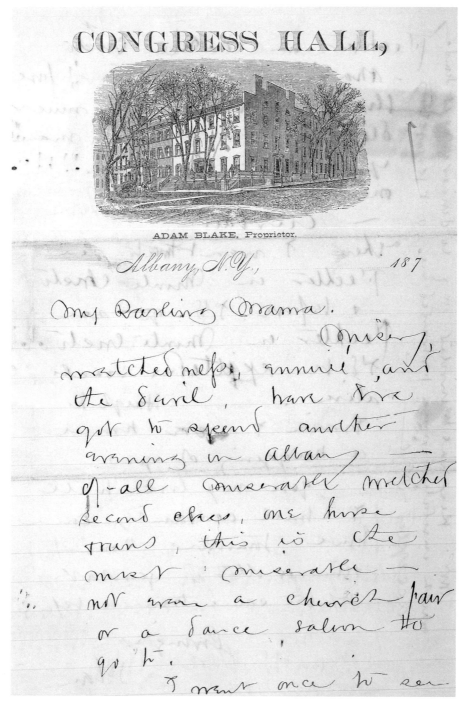

CONGRESS HALL,

ADAM BLAKE, Proprietor.

Albany, N.Y.,   187

My Darling Mama.

     Misery,
wretched ness, ennui, and
the devil, have I've
got to spend another
evening in Albany —
of-all miserable wretched
second class, one horse
towns, this is the
most miserable —
not even a church fair
or a dance saloon to
go to.
     I went once to see

To his mother, c. 1874

CHILDHOOD & APPRENTICESHIP

Stanford White wrote the first of these letters when he was a child visiting his father's relatives in Orange, New Jersey.

The next letters date from his apprenticeship to H. H. Richardson. White joined the firm, Gambrill & Richardson, in 1870, working under the supervision of the chief draftsman Charles Follen McKim. In 1872, shortly after the firm was awarded the commission to design Trinity Church in Boston, McKim resigned to start his own practice and Stanford White was put in charge of the project.

During this period Richardson sent him out of town to supervise various other projects, the Hampden County Courthouse in Springfield, Massachusetts, the State Capitol in Albany, and the State Asylum in Buffalo, New York, for example.

As a young man White often visited his maternal aunt Laura Fellows Mease, who lived near Newburgh, New York. From there he would roam about the Hudson River Valley and the Catskills, making exquisite sketches reminiscent of Turner. They show "an accurate eye and a nervous hand, and a deep sense of the poetry of landscape," as his son, Lawrence Grant White, observed.

South Street Seaport, New York

Study of a tree, 1866

ORANGE, NEW JERSEY. C. 1863

MY DEAR PAPA AND MAMA

I hope you all are well. I suppose that neither of you like to have me come back, as we are so dreadful. We have had a great deal of fun since we have been up here. I went black-berrying on Satterday and picked a quart of blackberries. Mr. Ackerman let us row him to Yonkers the day before yesterday. I have been in the watter a good many times and can swim 10 strokes but I can't keep my head out of watter. I am sleepy and cant write any more so good by love to all from your affectionate son, Stanford White

ORANGE, NEW JERSEY. C. 1865

DEAR MAMA,

In case We should not return on Monday, through cause of rain or sickness, I will write to you now. We arrived here all safe on Friday night and found all well.

We started our tramp on Monday morning, and had nice cool weather and a splendid time, of which I will tell you when I see you. We got back on Thursday all well and footsore, and sorry to say I had a chill yesterday. I am all well this morning, but I am afraid to come home, as I may have another chill, today, but I hope not and hope for the best. Dick is going to the salt meadows today, and poor me has got to stay home. Since we left you we have walked over a hundred miles; we have not received the map yet, so I suppose Papa forgot all about it. And now Dear Mama, hoping that you are all well I must bid you good bye.

From Your Affectionate Son, Stanford White
Dear Papa, if you want to read this note you can.

To his mother, c. 1865

BOSTON. OCTOBER 29, 1872

MY BELOVED MOTHER

Through the goodness of Beneficent Providence I am here—with an horrible influenza and bruised knee—in Boston.

Query? Whether—for my being here—I am to thank Providence or the Railway Time Table, I don't know; but to one or the other, most certainly, is

Sunset over Hudson Valley town

ascribable my bunged-up nose, and my banged up knee. Which, being translated into the mother tongue, means that—having started at the early hour of eight in the morning from Aunt Laura's, I have arrived in Boston, in the long-to-be-remembered and never-to-be-forgotten time of 28 hours, four and a half minutes.

Truly this is an age of progress and refinement!

Having wept over the glories of the Catskills, and gone into HYsterics over the HIGH pitched roofs in Albany, I took my seat in the Boston train, with the pleasant prospect of arriving in that city in time for a good night's sleep and a good supper. Behold the vanity of human aspirations! Fortune willed it that a cattle train (we being behind time) should start 5 minutes ahead of us at a certain place called Chester. For at this place there is one of those prides and glories of modern civilization—which, man having made, is so great, he must neither do reverence to God or the Bible, but to man's mind that conceived it—A trestle-work bridge? But this "creation" is as subject to nature's laws as anything else; and when a hot day and a cold night occur in the same 24 hours, whether it be made of wood and iron or iron alone, an unequal expansion sometimes occurs with disastrous consequence, which having occurred, and the unfortunate cattle train having started instead of us—it fell through—that is to say that part of it which could conveniently get on the bridge; and that part that was behind and was not on the bridge tumbled in after and that that was before jumped the track and went meandering about the country in a manner that was astonishing to behold.

Of course our train could not go on; and after waiting two hours with the prospect of waiting two days if we stayed where we were, it was decided to transfer us. We taking the up train on the other side of the bridge, and going down with it. To do so we had to walk about a quarter of a mile in the dark so I and my seat-fellow, with whom I had made acquaintance, offered our services to a party of ladies. He carrying the baby, and I escorting the ladies—the best part of the bargain you would have thought, they all being pretty—but wait. After having lifting them all down (it being about 4 ft. from our step to the ground) the man with the baby, going first, fell. I had the additional pleasure of carrying the youngest girl over what appeared to be a small puddle, but which lengthened out to be one of 300 paces. Now, it was very pleasant for the first hundred; but the last two? My shoulder doth cry out against it now. And I had no reward; for she, being of the tender age of 15, was so shy that she kept clear of me for the rest of the performance. And then she weighed enough to be 20!

When we got to the other station, what a sight met our eyes, and that sight continued continually during the long seven hours we waited for our train: trains going, liberated and mad steers lunging, the women consequently screaming and I catching cold, all at the rate of forty miles an hour. (Gracious me, there goes eleven o'clock!) The result of it was that after getting off the track twice, during which performances I got my knee bruised, I have got in Boston.

The flights of imagination, the bad writing, and the scratching out of words in this letter must all be attributed to a pen and paper, both equally bad.

Ever thy dutiful son, Stanford White

Barn, October 2, 1874

STANFORD WHITE

24

BOSTON. FEBRUARY 22, 1873

MY DEAR MOTHER,

I begin to think it is my fate—ill fate rather—to have neither peace of mind nor quiet of body. Both, I believe, quite necessary to man's happiness, tho seemingly not at all necessary to—Americans. Shirts—clean ones, that is—are also necessary, even to Yankees. I have none. But still feel quite happy in mind, being the contented possessor of a flag of a necktie, which I bought both to honor Washington, and hide my uncleanly linen.

Now don't get excited, nor send me any clothes. For, whatever is left of me—after the accidents which usually occur between Boston and Albany—will be in Buffalo, Wednesday morning 12.30. Sweet hour to arrive! With the probable thermometer at zero. This may be the result of fevered imagination—probably is. For, thanks to Richardson and his committees I feel as if I had been standing on my head all the week. Or, mayhap, champagne, which unteetotal-like, I—being depressed—drank for dinner.

However if you don't get another note from me, consider I'm in my right mind. How Richardson can be, I can't tell for, setting aside all brandies, gins, wines and cigars, it seems to me he chiefly subsists on boiled tripe, which he still insists on calling the "entrails of a cow." How's that?

I'm mad! Deuced mad. I wanted to go to Aunt Laura's. And I can't. However I'll ruin the firm on champagne lunches to make up for it. I wish Buffalo was in Jericho, and I home. I've no doubt it would be better for both of us. I will telegraph when I leave for B., probably Tuesday morning 8.30 train.

"And though with strange vaccilation. In the eyes of the watcher the morning cometh, and also the night, there is not one hour of human existence that moves not on towards the perfect day." I wish I could believe so; for I see only a sad fury.

Good night, dear Mother. I'm very tired and very sleepy. Give my love to Father and Dick; and tell Uncle Graham to read Ruskin more, and the newspapers less, and he'll get some reasonable idea of Political Economy.

Faithful thy Son, Stanford

SPRINGFIELD, MASSACHUSETTS. 1873

MY DEAR MOTHER,

Unlucky again, as you will perceive by enclosed tickets, now no use. All I lack is Uncle Graham's quarrel revolver, strawberries, cream, and sugar being in abundance.

The country is looking its extremest, the inhabitants happy at prospective corn, and your humble son d——d hot, d——d dusty, and bitten by mosquitoes to that extent ——! And yet I am not happy.

Ever thine, Stan

New England house

BROOKLINE, MASSACHUSETTS. 1874

MY DARLING MAMMA,

I find I am in for another week, and of good hard work too, I suppose—the which I do not mind, if I be let alone. We've been a whole week preparing for work—"organizing" Mr. R. calls it—and nothing done. Heighho! Patience is a virtue, I believe. I wish I was—I mean I wish I was patient. Virtue then would come in good time, at least that is the way I look at it. Anyway, I'd sooner be patient than virtuous; because then, you see, I could bear with fortitude my own sins, as well as other people's; and I could stand this "d—-d hot" day, and I wouldn't wish it was tomorrow, so I could go to work, or yesterday, so that I might go to bed earlier, and feel better today.

I suppose you think that patience would come with virtue. My dear mother, you never were so mistaken in all your life—besides, I don't mean that kind of virtue.

Where are them shirts—

If I didn't have to work so hard, and didn't want to get home—now there is another thing, I am never away from home two days, But (strange as it may seem to you) I'm deuced impatient to get back again, save I be going a-sketching in the mountains; now this destroys my peace and quiet, which of all—

Well, to return to my muttings, I was going to say I should like to stay here all— well, at least, till I had sketched half a dozen old houses, as many bends in the roads, and painted a valley at sunset—such a little valley—jingo, talk about the Pastoral Symphony!

A DELL

Where two meandering brooks doth meet
Lapping the stones that line the velvet swards,
Their joyful gurgling mingling with the rustling
leaves,
The o'erarching trees to mammoth heights are grown,
tossing their heads above,
While underneath, like sentinels doth stand
The slender trunks, companions of my solitude.
Over the hills and far away
Now sinks the King of Day to rest.
Over the hills and far away
Now, weary soul, can thou go to
Far away, beyond the hills,
Beyond the hills with the sinking sun,
And sink with the sun till it meets the night,
Till it meets the night so dark and drear;
Then rise with the stars and soar, O soul,
Then sit with the stars—give it up—
Devil! No more paper.
Ever thine, S.W.

NOTE

In 1874 Richardson moved to Brookline, Massachusetts, and opened an office in his house on Cottage Street. His partner, Charles Gambrill, remained in the New York office. Stanford White was based in New York but made frequent trips to Brookline, where he lived and worked in Richardson's house.

STANFORD WHITE

Mr R send his regards   Brookline
as I do my   Sunday Morning
love to you & all

My Darling Mamma.

            I find I am in for
another week have of good hard work
too I suppose, the which I do not
mind, if I be let alone.   We've
been a whole week preparing for what
"organizing" Mr R. calls it — + nothing
done   Heigho: Patience is a Virtue
I believe, I wish I was, — I mean
I wish I was patient — Virtue then
would come in good Time, at least
that is the way I look at it;   Any
way I'd sooner be patient than virtuous,
because, then you see, I could bear with

To his mother, 1874

CHILDHOOD & APPRENTICESHIP

27

Mill, Hudson Valley, New York

Bridge, Hudson Valley, New York

ALBANY, NEW YORK. C. 1876

MY DARLING MAMA,

Misery, wretchedness, ennui, and the devil—have I got to spend another evening in Albany? Of all miserable wretched second-class one-horse towns, this is the most miserable—not even a church fair or a dance saloon to go to.

I went once to see Fletcher in Monte Cristo— Aha! Thunder! Murder!!! You must die!! You're a dead man! Your hour has come!!! One! Two!! Three!!!

—Curtain—

Then I went twice to see Fletcher in Monte Cristo—and before I'd go again to see Fletcher in Monte Cristo, I'd be spitted and roasted alive. Heigh ho! How I wish I were home a-hugging of you.

Give my love to all. I shall certainly come home tomorrow some time, probably by the same train as before.

Lovingly, Stan

Mrs. Reynal has invited me to dinner next Sunday, which invitation was forwarded me, and I promptly accepted it.

GAMBRILL & RICHARDSON, ARCHITECTS
57 BROADWAY, NEW YORK
C. 1878

MY DARLING MAMA,

Your photograph was lovely, and has been very much admired. I am going to leave it with Mr. R.

Mine is simply damnable, and I will give it to no one. Expect me to breakfast on Tuesday morning and have it at sharp eight. I hope you are all well.

Lovingly, Stan

C. 1878

MY DEAR MAMA,

Much obliged—Hang Wescott's express. I think I certainly shall be back for Easter Tuesday or Wednesday—but may have to return here for another week. I am going down to pass the night with W. P. P. Longfellow, Longfellow's nephew, on Wednesday, and am going to Howell's and Charles Eliot Norton's later in the week.

I am glad to hear that you are better; you say nothing about Papa and Aunt Gussie, so I suppose they are all right, or the same as when I left. I am sorry I was not at Thomas' concert.

If you cannot like the Tristan and Isolde music, I am sorry for you. We are having pleasant weather here, but no clothes to wear.

How is Dick? When you write again let me know what he says. The Egg eval (?) Co, you may be sure, will bust up before I am off. Three months, and he will come kiting home, to comfort you for my absence.

Give all my love, and here are a thousand kisses from your son, Stan

NOTE

William Pitt Preble Longfellow (1836–1913), architect who designed the Boston Post Office; later on the architecture faculty at MIT.

William Dean Howells (1837–1920), novelist and editor-in-chief of the Atlantic Monthly.

Charles Eliot Norton (1827–1908), editor of the North American Review *(1862–68) and professor of art history at Harvard University (1873–97).*

View across the Hudson Valley

BUFFALO, NEW YORK.

MY DEAR MOTHER,

To think after insuring my life for $3000 I am here all safe! It's disgraceful. I came pretty near it, though. Left Boston at 9 p.m. Tuesday in the beastliest sleeping car it has been my lot to inhabit. The train was long, too, being composed of one car and the engine. We were about half way to Albany when the engine burst one of her pistons; and a fat woman opposite me kicked up such a hullabaloo that I couldn't get to sleep till daylight. I then took the Pacific Express and arrived here at 1 o'clock in the morning, in an awful state of being.

I propose to do the Falls, or as much of them as can be did in two hours. So if you don't hear any more of me, just remember that the no. of my Ins. ticket is 419, agent 340. If Mr. Richardson don't join me, I shall be in a state of bankruptcy. So if I telegraph you, just send me a check and I'll pay it back as soon as I get home. There is no possible danger of it, however. Will probably be home Wednesday or Saturday.

Your loving son, Stanford

STANFORD WHITE

Lake Mohonk, from Overlook, New York

EUROPEAN TOUR

White wrote these letters during his sketching tour in Europe. He had resigned from his position as a draftsman for Richardson and had not yet joined Charles Follen McKim and William Rutherford Mead to form McKim, Mead & White.

White sailed for France, accompanied by McKim, on the *Perière* on July 3, 1878. On arrival in Paris they were warmly received by Augustus Saint-Gaudens and his wife. The Exposition Universelle had opened in the spring, drawing many of their colleagues in the arts to Paris. White writes to his mother that he divided his first days in Europe between visiting the Exposition and exploring the city.

With Paris as a base, White made a number of trips to various regions of France. In May 1879 he went to Italy and ended his journey in London in August. Both the detail and length of the letters and the profusion of sketches convey his enthusiasm for all he saw, not only for architecture, but also for painting and sculpture.

McKim and Saint-Gaudens, his traveling companions on the trip down the Rhône, became his lifelong friends and associates. Saint-Gaudens, in his *Reminiscences*, describes the friendship of "the three redheads," noting his acquaintance with McKim was based on a "a devouring love for ice cream."

Church at Breval, September 20, 1878

Stanford White, c. 1877–78

STANFORD WHITE

34

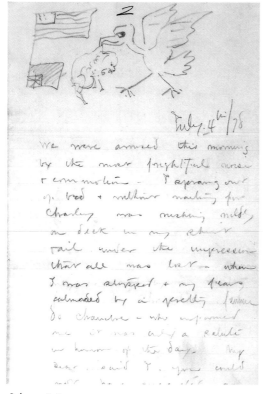

July 4, 1878

ON BOARD THE PERIÈRE. JULY 3, 1878

DEAR MAMA,

The last signs of "mine own countrie" passed away
without emotion on my part, as I was engaged in
guzzling Seltzer water with McKim in the *salle à
manger,* and came up on deck only to find the limit-
less ocean for an horizon. The weather is superb, the
vessel runs on an even keel, McKim and myself are in
splendid stomach and spirits and what time we are
not eating the manifold meals they provide us with
on this good ship, we are drinking your health and

happiness in Seltzer (also Tarrant), Vichy, soda, vin
rouge, champagne, cognac, and Chartreuse verte.
Talking about "Tarrant," a sallow and dyspeptic-look-
ing Yankee came up while we were enjoying our bottle, and with a preface that he was looking for a
"purgative" offered to buy ours at a high price. It suf-
fices to say that we referred him to the ship Doctor,
and he has not been heard of since. I suppose a com-
pound cathartic was too much for him.

We passed the *Amérique* inward bound— just
opposite the forts. There was immediately a tremendous commotion aboard: two boatswains and at least
20 men made an endeavor to signal her—which
effort was entirely frustrated by the total loss of the
halyards amidst a frightful amount of cursing and
swearing.

No one could wish a better ship; she is a fine vessel, and very fast, bouncing along at the rate of 15
knots an hour. The Captain is a thorough gentleman,
and I am sure, sailor—and he is quiet, even to stern-
ness. The First Officer likewise, and the Purser jolly
and handsome. The crew might be better, and as for
the passengers—Good God! —and good night.

JULY 4

We were aroused this morning by the most frightful noise and commotion. I sprang out of bed, and
without waiting for Charlie was rushing wildly on
deck in my shirt tail under the impression that all was
lost, when I was stopped, and my fears calmed, by a
pretty *femme de chambre* who informed me that it was
only a salute in honor of the day. My dear, said I, you
could not have suggested a thing more to my mind.
*Permettez-moi? "Non, non, monsieur, et mon Dieu, quel
costume!"* I suddenly became aware of my shirt tail,
and rushed as frantically back as I had out, to find

McKim adjusting a life preserver to his body, and wanting to know what the H— was the matter. It will take us some time to get accustomed to the French way of handling a ship.

We are having a most beautiful run of weather—the wind is on our quarter and there is no motion whatever. McKim is in high spirits at his freedom from sickness of any kind. The passengers are briefly McKim and myself: the others amount to nothing. They are Spaniards, Central Americans, Cubans, 2nd Class French people, and 100th. Class Americans; and yet, let me make an exception in the persons of the Archbishop of Sydney and his assistant, monsieur l'abbé. The archbishop is like one of Holbein's prelates, round fat jolly and sleek, with a soft eye and small mouth and benignant smile; his hair is white as the snow, and I am sure his life, also. His assistant is entirely a different type of man, who, although he eats and drinks as heartily as any one at the table, has evidently lived a life of self-abnegation, and a happy one. He is very tall and slim, and has an intensely intellectual face. The contrast is amusing. [sketch]

Alas! They can "spike" but little English. Mons. l'abbé greets me in the morning with: "Ah! How you is? *Très bien?* How you sleep?" McKim, by the way, is an evil brute. He engages in conversation with all the passengers around and leaves me to starve, because I dare not ask for anything in bad French and not a damn waiter understands English. *Tiens, tiens,* the laugh will come on him as soon as we strike rough water. Bye bye for today.

JULY 5

Somewhat of a sea today, but still hardly worth speaking of. Nothing, however, will assure a few ladies aboard that death is not near at hand. The tables are not so full either, for which I thank heaven, as my appetite is voracious, and it gives me a better chance. I am also lazy, and as nothing of importance has turned up, I will shut up. Adieu.

JULY 6

Fourth day. Wind dead ahead; sky overcast; pitching somewhat. Steamer chairs chiefly to let. Have just run into the Banks. Heretofore have worn summer clothes and no overcoat, and slept under nothing. It is now very chilly, and I am the only one without an overcoat. Great Heavens!—Oh Lord, I have just returned from deck—they are blowing something they call a "fog syren"—to such a blast must the souls of the damned be awakened to eternal torture. It puts an end to this.

DINNER TIME

The ladies (sic? or rather sick) have chiefly deserted us, except a few staunch old sailors. Fog has lifted. We just passed a steamer; who do you think she was? "To Hell with You" of the National Line! Wasn't it funny! Ugh! There she goes, into the fog again, Good bye, good night, and God bless you.

JULY 7

Steward! Garçon! garçon! Vite! G—D—! Sapristi! *Dépêchez vous!* [sketch] ugh!

ugh!!! Last night about one o'clock, the vessel commenced pitching [sketch] most violently, and the howl of sick arose and would not be hushed. I heeded them not, but bent all my energies to keeping myself from being pitched out of my berth; and have so far succeeded that I am now writing this after breakfast. It is too hard work, however, so I will wai . . . . t until tomorrow, if the ship is still afloat.

We are in what sailors call the Devil's Hole, and a devil of a hole it is. It was only what sailors call "fresh weather" yesterday. The sea really was not very heavy, but directly abeam, and the consequence was that we bobbed around in the trough of the sea in a most appalling manner. The only one of three men who sat at my table at breakfast (and who came there by the way in his night shirt, with his trousers and coat over it, having made a vain and unsuccessful attempt to dress) observed that this was "the most G——D——tub for rolling he ever was in"—evidently the remark of a sea-sick man. The racks have been up since yesterday morning—nor do they prevent the soup, wine, and dishes from landing occasionally in our laps. [sketches] All this does not prevent me from eating the most huge meals.

Yesterday I ate the following, to the disgust of my somewhat sea-sick neighbor, and the amazement of the waiter:

Little Clams	Salad
Sago soup	Roast Pigeons
Radishes	Gruyere Cheese
Veal Croquettes	Pudding Imperial
Spanish Mackerel	Blackberries
Roasted Kidneys	Cake National
Broiled Chicken	Nuts and Raisins
Roast Beef	Coffee

The entire Menu!

We passed close to four ships. [sketch] They looked splendid in the sea. The sea rose at times 15 feet higher than our vessel, but so far we have only shipped two of them, as the wind is dead astern—having changed about midday yesterday. Otherwise we should all be dead men.

I have had but two hours sleep in the last 48. Spent last night in the smoking room, as we are all battened down, and the air in our stateroom was per-

McKim aboard the Perière

fectly intolerable. Today it is much less rough.

McKim since yesterday has been past a joke. He assumed the attitude here depicted [sketch] early in the morning, and only left it late at night to go to bed, with the exception of most copious tributes to Neptune. Once while he was dragging out his existence, the Second Officer passed. Monsieur, said he, do you think this sort of thing will continue? No, said the officer, no. It is very fine weather, but it cannot last long. Immediate collapse of McKim—

Perière passenger

only to be brought to by unlimited application of chloral trioxide(?), prescribed by the doctor, to whom he applied at once.

MONDAY

Storm abating; McKim picking up. Nothing has happened. Good night.

TUESDAY

It is my turn now. Not sea sickness, but stomach ache. I think I took cold last night. Why oh why did you not put Valpeau in the bag?

WEDNESDAY

All right. One week at sea, and getting pretty tired of it. The portholes have been closed for three days, and the air in our room is almost noisome. I get up unrefreshed every morning, and I am afraid this will interfere with getting fat. There is nothing to write about except the passengers—the old bishop and abbé I have told you about. At my left sits an old French woman who is a very pleasant and joky companion, and must have been howling pretty once. She says anything, and is willing to have anything said to her. At my right a German with a big nose; McKim opposite the old French woman, and Mons. l'abbé opposite me.

One could write a book on the ship's company. There are an assortment of Cook's tourists aboard who, what time they are not throwing up, violently endeavor to learn French. They are in the tow of a Professor, who alternately teaches them French and gives unattended lectures to the passengers. His name is Prof. Narcisse Cyr, and he is a great donkey. Indeed the genus ass has too many varieties aboard to describe them all. The man (Lyons by name) who was on the lookout for a purgative exceeds them all. He mauls the French language most horribly, carries 16 pocket dictionaries, and when he can get no one to talk to—like Demosthenes on the beach—he spouts French to the sea, and answers himself back again. And then—oh, then—there is a man—an old man—hot from Noah's Ark—who nevertheless has never been outside of Massachusetts—who has never heretofore had any yearnings but for beans, and more beans. What in the name of goodness should have put into this old fellow's head a trip to Paris and the

Alps, beats the Dutch, and us too. He is one of the Cooks tourists, and a most ardent student of French; but as yet has mastered only one sentence: *"très bien."* But at no matter what hour you get up or at what hour you go to bed, you see him poring over his books. He follows the professor like a shadow and is his most promising student. The rig that he gets himself up in is beyond description.

An old army cap of '48, a shawl twice too big for him, and a shamble like a sick cow. [sketch] He is the butt of the whole ship's company, who fire French at him till he is nearly wild. Enough of this—I am afraid I have taxed your patience too much already, and am pretty tired myself.

I have made one or two good friends, the Pollocks and Duncans of Washington and N.Y.—very nice people. There are three pretty Spaniards aboard, but alas they can speak nothing but their own tongue. We sight land tomorrow and land the night after, if all goes well. Till then, adieu.

FRIDAY

Hooray! Old England on our lee. Bless her! Too much excitement aboard to write.

We have just taken our French pilot aboard, and also, ha! ha! some fresh mackerel. Shall not sight France until dark, and will arrive about midnight. Dinner in Paris tomorrow.

Good bye. Be sure to write me everything. Number your letters, so I can be sure I miss none. I will pay up in my next for the ungodly length of this! I shall have to post this immediately on landing, perhaps before. So good bye again, love and a thousand kisses from your loving son

[Signed with monogram]

Perière passenger

Alley in Bernay

STANFORD WHITE

PARIS. JULY 18, 1878

MY DEAREST MOTHER,

I am at present domiciled in the sky parlor of a very pleasant "tinniment" in the Latin Quarter—No 1, rue de Fleurus. We overlook the Palace and Gardens of the Luxembourg, and most beautiful gardens they are—certainly the most beautiful I have ever seen. Indeed, in all Paris, we could not wish for a better situation. We have a large and a small bed and hall etc., for which we pay 30 francs a week.

One's impressions of Paris are so varied that it would be next to impossible to sift them down into one or two sentences; but so far I have seen but little to dislike, and much to go into wild admiration about. It fully meets my expectations in every regard, save *"Bal de Nuit."*

I have been going on one continuous hum ever since I got here, and it must be a dispensation of Providence that gives me a moment to write this letter. McKim is prancing up and down impatiently in the next room, which forces me to be as short as possible. Briefly then, we are both in good health and spirits, are satisfied with everything and everybody and are generally having as good a time as it is possible for us to have—with the exception that we both are horribly virtuous—so far.

We landed in Havre Saturday in a hard rain which very kindly stopped before we started for breakfast. Oh such a breakfast! Our long sea voyage had tuned our appetites to the key of fresh green vegetables and fruit, and we played upon it to purpose; nothing ever tasted so good before. We took breakfast and came on to Paris with the Duncans and the Pollocks, with whom we are now fast and intimate friends. The journey to Paris was delightful beyond description, as far as the scenery went—but we were so tired we could not enjoy it. We arrived in Paris at half past four and went to the Hotel Corneille.

I must close this quickly—as it is it may not catch the mail. Everything about clothes all right, and I have found the little sewing case of immense use. We both blessed you also for the camphor. Direct your letters to Baring Bros. or rather Hottinguer & Co, Paris until otherwise advised. Yours and Dick's letters just received. Love to all; will write by Thursday's mail if possible.

Ever ever ever yrs,

[Signed with monogram]

House in Toulouse

View of Arras

Gate to Arras

PARIS. JULY 20, 1878

MY DARLING MOTHER,

To take up the thread of my discourse, we first went to the Hotel Corneille Saturday afternoon, and took rooms at the enormous rate of 2f50 per diem, a head. It is not a good hotel in any way, but one of the best in the Latin Quarter. We then went to dinner (after arranging ourselves)—at Foyot's, the crack restaurant of the student quarter and one of the best in Paris. It may have been that my appetite was keen and sharpened by the days of steamer fare—but all the grub that I had ever eaten before seemed but poor stuff to this. We had soup, fish, filet aux pommes, petits pois, salade, cheese, strawberries, coffee and wine, at the cost of 6 francs 50 apiece. We then took a long bath at a public bath-house—we had the water changed two or three times and left about a quarter of an inch of ourselves behind.

It was too late to do any bumming, so, being very tired, we wisely went to bed.

Yesterday (Saturday) closed my first week in Paris. It would be useless to attempt to describe what I did, even in so short a time. Impressions, comparisons, how I like this (and I usually did), how I didn't like that, would be as likely to fill a hundred pages as ten—the limit of every respectable letter. Here, therefore, is a condensed diurnal account, with foot-notes "ad lib."

Sunday. In the morning, I have a dim idea that we did not get up until about midday, but am not sure. However we went to church in the afternoon (St. Germain-des-Près, a 12th century church) and to the theater, like bad boys, in the evening. The church on the whole was the more interesting of the two. Yet it really was the play that was at fault and not the theater

(I forgot to say it was the Théatre Français) nor the actors—both surpassing my expectations. We had a lively little comedy first, beautifully played, — and then an infernally classic tragedy by Racine called "Phèdre" in which Mme Sh. Bernhart played magnificently. The evening's entertainment was rounded off, after midnight, by a pretty little farce but we were tired to death, and did not enjoy it. Here are the footnotes running over two pages. I must chop them off.

Monday morning. Roamed around Paris—went to the "Salon of '78," which is not at all interesting, in the afternoon. In the evening to the "Opéra Comique" and saw Herold's "Pré aux Clercs," a most lovely little opera, and the most perfect performance I have ever seen. The opera debouched itself about midnight, and we then went—!!!!! to the "Mabile"!! Shudder not, my dear mama, for we left in twenty minutes—two very disgusted men.

Tuesday. Stratton joins us, and from this time forward we are three. Paris in the morning, exposition in the afternoon; "Bouffes" in the evening; "Bullier," the students' ball, after midnight.

Wednesday. Paris in the morning, exposition in the afternoon; dinner with Armstrong, St. Gaudens, Stratton and Greenough, the sculptor's son, in the evening.

Thursday. The Louvre in the morning, the exposition in the afternoon, and in the evening, dined with Mr. Robt. Lennox Kennedy, with whom Stratton is traveling.

Friday. Paris, Exposition etc., and to the concert in the "Orangerie" in the evening.

Saturday. Versailles; Sunday, I am now writing.

You see we have been pretty busy. The "Bals de Nuit," I am both glad and sorry to say, are pretty

poor performances. Vice, I suppose, is the same all the world over; but I am ashamed to say I had hoped to find it in a less offensive—and, well, more pleasing form here. Pleasing or not, you need not fear: I do not think I shall go to one again.

The Exposition is very much like ours: a little larger and more grandiose, but not much better, save in the French Department and the Fine Arts. As far as pictures go, it is by far the greatest exhibition of modern paintings ever held. They date from about 1850 to the present time, and include all the important works of the best men of all countries.

It is horribly tiresome work, both at the Exposition and elsewhere, and I shall be almost glad when we start for the country, which will be next Saturday, or Monday.   Everything is comparatively cheap here, except "dwelling"; and then again you are charged for everything: napkins, ice, etc., which is exceedingly aggravating. The necessities of life are sadly neglected, and French cleanliness consists solely of washing one's face and hands, and putting on clean linen—where it shows. What a pity it is that we cannot go abroad and yet stay at home at the same time! I wish you were over here too—it seems horribly selfish to be going on all these bats. However they will only last 6 or 7 days longer, and then hard work and cheap restaurants. I am afraid this letter won't catch the post either. Good bye, love to all, and a thousand kisses from your loving son

[Signed with monogram]

NOTE

Sidney V. Stratton, architect and a close friend of McKim (both trained in the atelier of Honoré Daumet in Paris); associated with McKim, Mead & White during the early 1880s.

David Maitland Armstrong (1836-1918), painter and worker in stained glass; director of the American Department of the Exposition Universelle. Among his major works were the stained glass for the chapel at Biltmore House and St. Paul's Chapel at Columbia University and the mosaics for the Villard Houses.

Alfred Greenough, son of sculptor Richard Saltonstall Greenough (1819-1904).

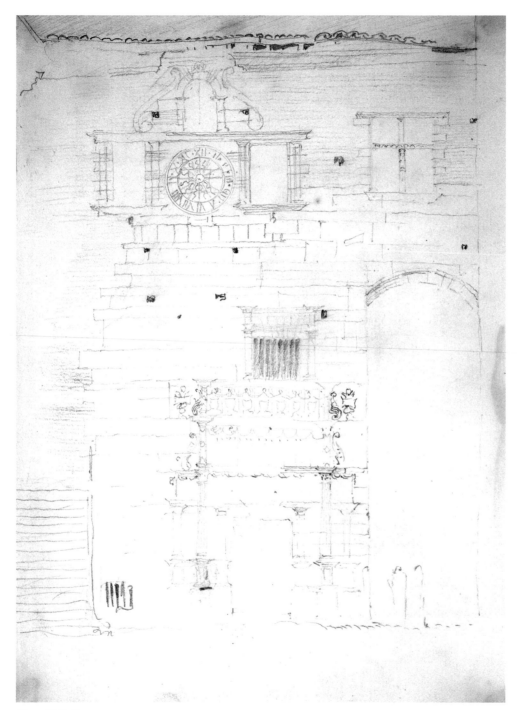

Town Hall, France

PARIS. AUGUST 2, 1878

DEAR MAMA,

As usual my letter writing must be pushed to the wall. I am way behind in packing and we are off to the South of France this afternoon.

Yours of the 14th enclosing a letter from Aunt Laura received.

Of course I can hope nothing about Aunt Gussie, but it makes me feel wretched to think of the hard time you must be having and that I am not there to help you. Give her my best love if she is alive when this reaches you. If not, Heaven's will be done.

Please try and get all the rest you can by going up to Aunt Laura's. I will write there as soon as I get back to Paris.

There is nothing new to tell you about our movements — we haven't been to the theatre much lately and have been going through the same routine in the daytime as before. We leave by this afternoon's 3:05 train for Fontainebleau and go on successively to Sens, Dijon, Lyons, Avignon, Nimes, Le Puy, Clermont, Bourges, etc., and back to Paris, arriving there in 11 to 14 days. If you do not get a letter from me for ten days do not be frightened. I may not get your letters either until I get back to Paris but I think I shall.

Love to all. Do not tire yourself and get all the rest you can.

Ever lovingly yr son, Stan
I am in good health and feeling splendidly

PARIS. MID-AUGUST, 1878

DEAREST MOTHER,

No. 4 received at Bourges just after writing my last and No. 5 of August 2nd yesterday on my return here.

By the time this reaches you I hope poor Aunt Gussie's suffering will be over—but I cannot rid myself of the feeling that I ought to be with you helping you instead of over here.

Do all you can to keep well and don't write me false accounts of how you are. I hope you will go up to Newburgh and stay a month or two as soon as it is possible.

I am a very ungrateful boy. I discovered the bottle of Valpeau one day when I did not want it. Since then it has been mashed in my bag with direful result. Luckily one shirt and two pocket handkerchiefs took most of the dose—with what effect I have not been able to judge yet as they have not yet come back from the *Blanchisseuse.*

I am getting to be tired already of writing "accounts" of what I see and so will blow off one d___ long account of my trip to the South of France, which, after having endeavored to read at home, you can pass around to the Caseys "Up the River," Dick and anybody else you choose.

The weather here continues most lovely and cool. We are both well and as happy as circumstances will allow.

We start on the 20th or 21st for a ten days trip in Brittany.

McKim sends regards. Keep well and write often.

Love to all and a thousand kisses from your loving son

[Signed with monogram]

La Bonneville, September 22, 1878

We three, viz.—Charles F. McKim, secretary of the American Institute of Architects, Honorary member—etc.—etc.—Aug. St. Gaudens, sculptor of great renown, and your dutiful son—secretary of nothing, of no renown whatever, started Friday afternoon Aug. the 2nd for a grand flank movement on the South of France—which we made in the following order, taking each town without opposition, and leaving them (with one exception) with great regret.

Paris, Fontainebleau, Moret, Sens, Dijon, Beaune, Lyons, Lyons down the Rhône to Avignon, Arles, St. Gilles, Tarascon, Nîmes, Langogne across the mountains by diligence to, Le Puy, Issoire, Clermont, Riom, Moulins, Bourges, Tours, Blois, and back to Paris by way of Orleans.

Fontainebleau is too well known to describe. The grounds are very pretty, and the castle has quite a homelike air, almost all of the large chateaux looking more like public buildings than places to live in.

Moret was a lovely little walled town (with old gate towers, and old church, and a little river running past them) dirty and decayed—Sens was dirty and decayed without being lovely but with a very fine cathedral, and Dijon not only had a very fine cathedral but for a wonder—was both clean and cheerful. We spent Sunday there and went to church three or four times.

At Beaune, besides the beauty of the town itself, we came across two very attractive and inseparable things, viz.—good wine and pretty women—but, *mon dieu!* all dressed up in high heeled boots and Paris fashions. The town is still encircled by its old walls, crowned with machicolations and guarded by round towers. The gates were destroyed by Henry IV and the moat has now become one continuous vegetable garden. We took a bottle of old Beaune into the railway carriage (which we had to ourselves) and I think became quite tight before getting to Lyons.

Lyons is the second (modern) city in France—a sort of third rate Paris—and a more uninteresting place it would be impossible to imagine. Oh! là là! I have forgotten the principal thing in Beaune, better even than its old music and young women—viz. the Hotel Dieu, built in 1450 and in perfect working order now. Indeed one would almost wish to fall sick, to get in such a hospital. Though four hundred years old, it was clean and sweet, and the court—with an old well and new orange trees—as quiet as a cloister.

It is in [the] charge of a company of white nuns with cheerful faces and absolutely spotless linen. We were received with the utmost courtesy, and welcomed into the grand old kitchen by a fair sister, with her sleeves rolled up to her shoulders, and a huge soup ladle in her hand.

And now, having taken leave of Beaune, let us pass Lyons in silence and imagine us sailing swiftly on the "bosom" of the finest river in France.

Setting aside architectural reasons, this was by far the most interesting part of our voyage. The trip down the Rhône is very rarely made now by travelers. The boats go but once a week and then again, it is sometimes very dangerous.

The character of the scenery in some places is quite like that of the Hudson and in parts finer—notably when the Alps and Mt. Blanc (eighty miles off) come into view, and then the river is crammed with old castles and towns and surrounded by histories and traditions, which give every part of it an

interest of its own. Here I am getting into a second class guide book way of writing.

We were routed out of bed at the unearthly hour of five, and driven down to the boat with the general desire to punch the heads of everybody and hotel people in particular. For why—I mean for why were we routed up at five? Because we had to be at the boat half an hour before it started, and it didn't start till half an hour after time. In France they set the clocks in front of the railway stations ten minutes in advance, so everybody shall come early; and the clocks inside the station ten minutes behind hand, so no one shall be left. Well, down we get to the boat half an hour ahead of time, and find everything in an uproar, the boat getting up steam in the most violent manner, the captain swearing and about ten men trying to haul a sack of oats aboard. Meanwhile during all this fuss the grand old river is sweeping past us at its incredible pace, the sun has begun to dispel the fog, a small boy under the mistaken impression that we are going to start gets up on the paddle wheel and commences to toot on a French Bugle. Suddenly there appears on top of the hill an old woman and boy, the woman carrying a bedstead and the boy a chair, and waves them wildly around as a signal to the captain that she wants to get aboard, which was entirely unnecessary as the captain has no intention of starting for the next ten minutes. Nevertheless he and all the rest of the crew and passengers get up and gesticulate to her to hurry up or she will be left. Gotten aboard safely, she bats the boy over the head, for something he has not done, rolls the bedstead over the toes of half the passengers, and disappears (cursing loudly) in the cabin. The cabin has become quite full and it is a long time after the time for start-

ing; but the captain still lingers on in the hope of catching another passenger, who however not appearing, he at last waves his hand to the engineer to start, the lines are cast off. Toot tootle toot toot too goes the small boy, we madly fight the current for ten minutes, and then—whiz—around we go and are under and past the first bridge before you can say Jack Robinson.

The boat is 275 ft. long and not over 20 ft. wide, *comme ça*. [sketch] She holds about two hundred people, with beds and bagging unlimited, who also bring their grub, although there is a restaurant aboard.

The Rhône at no place is wider than the East River, but its color and the tremendous pace at which it flows gives it a character not easily forgotten. It must go at the rate of anywhere from eight to fifteen miles an hour. We made the whole distance between Lyons and Avignon—167 miles—within 12 hours, and they sometimes do it in nine. It takes them between two and three days to get back.

Down we go past mountains, hills, and towns— shooting bridges in an appalling manner and having hard work to stop at the wharfs, which we always manage to do, however, to the tootling of the small boy. At St. Peray McK rushes off the boat and invests in two bottles of sparkling wine, for which it is famous. We carry our prizes down into the cabin, under the impression that we are going to have a good breakfast—which impression is somewhat dimmed by the waiter informing us that they had forgotten the knives and forks. These, however, mysteriously appear. We "mange bien" and drink our wine, and when we reappear on deck, the river seems to flow faster, the mountains almost to move around;

Zuck Robinson

The boat is 275 ft l[ong]
& not over 20 ft wide "[...]"

She holds about two hun[dred]
people, with beds & baggage a[nd]
who also bring their grub, a[nd]
there is a restaurant aboard.

The Rhône at no p[oint]
is wider than the Sac[ramento]
River, but its color [and]
& the tremendous pace
which it flows, gives [it]
a character not easily
forgotten. It mus[t]
go at the rate of any w[here]
from eight to fifteen mi[les]
an hour. We made
the whole distance bet[ween]
Lyons & Avignon — 167. mi[les]

Sketch of the Rhône steamer

STANFORD WHITE

50

and the boat lurches from side to side in a fearful manner. We curl ourselves up in the sun, on the bow, and vow France "ish mosh magnificent countrish we ever saw." At Pont St. Esprit, we passed a grand old stone bridge of 20 arches, 2000 ft. long built in the 13th century by a company of monks. It took forty years to build, and up to this century was the largest stone bridge in the world. Just below this we made, with difficulty, a landing, and as we swing off, a fierce back eddy grabs us, whirls us around, and runs us neatly aground on an island. There is an immediate uproar, everybody shouts, the engineer leaves his engine and rushes on deck, the captain jumps off the boat and violently endeavors (this is really true) to push off a steamer 275 feet long with 200 passengers on it; and all this while the small boy keeps up his tootle te toot toot toot on the paddle box.

Between the sagacity of the helmsman and the force of the river our stem is gradually swung off, and we go on our way rejoicing again. The day all through was of the most perfect description and we arrived safely at Avignon (which towered up from the river like a rock) in the evening, found a very good hotel, had a most excellent dinner and a fine old bottle of Hermitage.

Avignon was the residence of the popes for two hundred years and has the largest and most grandiose medieval castle in the world, which is now used as a barracks.

It was by far the most impressive town we were in. At St. Gilles—a little out of the way town—(with the best piece of architecture in France in it, the triple marble porch of the church)—we were taken in charge by the abbé, who seemed delighted to come across some educated people, his flock (which he evi-

dently ruled with a rod of iron) being of the most ignorant description. He was very pleasant, but a little too priestly—his sole object in life being the restoration of his church—which God forefend. It was destroyed by the Huguenots and all the noses knocked off the saints and I hope they have been well boiled for it. He took occasion to give us his opinion of Huguenots in particular and Protestants in general, which would not have been in the very best taste, but for the slight touch of humor in it.

He presented us all with the medal of St. Gilles and took us over to his house which Pope Clement Fourth had lived in. At Arles the women are very pretty and their costume divine, all black and white with black and white head-dresses—nothing, however, to come up to St. Thegonnec in Brittany.

Nîmes is a very beautiful city and quite a thriving one. We took a bath in a splendid swimming-bath in water of the Rhône (nearly thirty miles away) brought by an old Roman aqueduct. There are all manner of old Roman theatres, amphitheatres, baths, etc., lying around loose in Nîmes and Arles. The amphitheatre at Nîmes is the most perfect in the world after Verona—they are having bullfights in it now. It seated 20,000 people. We sat on the top row of seats and imagined ourselves ancient Romans, and then I went down (while McKim and St. Gaudens stayed on top) and rushed madly into the arena, struck an attitude, and commenced declaiming. They heard me perfectly. I stabbed five or six gladiators and rushed out with the guardian in hot pursuit.

At Nîmes we sighted the Mediterranean and turned our faces sorrowfully homeward.

(SEPTEMBER 12TH, PARIS)

I have let six mails go past without finishing this

letter, and am going to take time by the forelock now and rush it through.

Our journey from Nîmes to Langogne was through a wild and mountainous country, the train at one time reaching an altitude of 3000 feet. The post roads, however, in the most savage parts are as good as those in Central Park. At Langogne we got on top of the stage coach and rolled over the mountain tops to Le Puy, a distance of about 35 miles. The scenery was quite like that of the Catskills. We passed through the highest village in France nearly 4000 ft. above the sea.

The sun had set before we landed in Le Puy, but a cold premonitory shudder went down our back bones as we trotted into the town. Le Puy is situated in quite a large valley, and is perhaps the most strikingly peculiar town in France, its peculiarity consisting in the rising of two great steep peaks right out of the midst of the town. [sketch] (I send you a photograph of one) Some of its old noble families still live there. On the whole, of all low, dirty, nasty, ill smelling, filthy, buggy places—that I have come across, Le Puy exceeds them all. The very remembrance of it makes me shudder. There is a great big hideous tin Virgin (56 ft. high) on top of the largest rock in Le Puy, whose sole object seems to be the utter destruction of the landscape for miles around. From Le Puy to Clermont, Caesar's Commentaries, I believe, would serve as a very good guide book. Clermont is the capital of Auvergne and is surrounded by (once) volcanic mountains, but in an hour's journey we are in Touraine—back again— thank heaven in the North of France. No more will we have to pull our beds on the floor before going to sleep, or leave one inn in the morning—silently

cursing it and its proprietor—with the gloomy feeling that the next one that we stop at may be worse. Not so. At Tours (otherwise not a very interesting place and full of English) we are driven into the prettiest of courts, and met by the loveliest of landladies, who smiles at us in the softest way and makes us feel that it is our personal comfort and nobody else's, which she has at heart.

Somehow or other I couldn't find my room three or four times, and had to go downstairs to ask her where it was and, strange as it may seem, met McKim and St. Gaudens on the same errand.

We are now in the valley of the Loire, and surrounded by magnificent old châteaux. Here the best French in France is spoken, and here the court held high revelry during the 15th, 16th, and 17th centuries to its ultimate annihilation.

As I am coming down here again, I won't bother you with describing it now, but will hurry you back to Paris with me to take a turkish bath, put on clean clothes, once again dine at Foyot's, and almost feel as if I was at home. For in spite of its wickedness, I am getting to have the appreciation which all good Americans have for Paris, and shall leave it for the last time with sorrow in my heart.

As I have now been through nearly 2,000 miles of France, I can begin to form some comparison between the railway travel here and with us, and after much profound cogitation have come to the following solemn conclusion. If you have a coupe (i.e. the front carriage, with a great bow-window in front) to yourself, I like it better than our drawing room cars. If you have a 1st. class carriage to yourself I like it as well as our D. R. cars, but if you don't have the carriage to yourself, it isn't as nice. The same way with

Cabrières. We passed through the highest village in France nearly 4000 above the sea.

The sun had set before we landed in Le Puy : but a cold premonitory shudder went down our back bones as we trotted in the town.

Le Puy is situated in quite a large valley, + is perhaps the most strikingly peculiar town in France.

Its peculiarality, consisting in the rising of two great steep rocks right out of the midst of the town. (I send you a photograph of one)

Le Puy.

Some of its old noble Families still

Sketch of Le Puy

the second class, if you have the voiture to yourself (which very rarely happens) it is better than our ordinary cars—if you don't, it is worse.

The third-class carriages are pens, although you meet some very polite people in them. The trains do not travel as quickly as with us, and they are never on time. They never have any accidents however and never run over anybody, which I suppose makes up for the absurd amount of red tape and fussing you have to go through to do anything or get anything done.

They are way behind us in the way of baggage.

The weather was absolutely perfect the whole time we were gone. We found the hotels tolerable (save in cleanliness) and the "cuisine" most excellent, except in one or two places. We had the utmost abundance of splendid fruit, and one of the pleasantest things on the journey was that we changed cheeses and wines at almost every town we came to. And such cheese, and oh! such wine—it would make even the nose of my skeptical uncle turn red with the smelling of it.

The people were uniformly kind and polite, and uniformly lied; and the further south you got, the politer they became and the more they lied—but what of that—and yet a good deal. If a person were suddenly transported from the south of France, with its fair skies, its fruit, wines and—suave (how do you spell it?) people whom you cannot trust—to Brittany,

where the sky is always gray, where there is no wine, but where the people though rough are absolutely honest, so honest that they call even their cousins the Normans a pack of liars—I say if he were transported from one place to the other, it wouldn't take him long to decide which he would sooner have, the politeness and lying, or the roughness and honesty.

So, to this day, the Bretons—though woefully behind on the subject of steam ploughs, Paris high heeled boots, and patent medicines—are true to their church and loyal to their sovereign, both by a great many people considered crimes in France now-a-days.

Liberté, Egalité, Fraternité—everywhere you see it planked even over the church doors. Pretty soon there will come another row—let us hope, then, that it will be wiped off again.

If you think that anybody else would like to wade through this note beside yourself and those at home, please send it to them.

Ever thy loving son,
[Signed with monogram]

NOTE

The portal of the twelfth-century church of Saint Gilles, which White describes as "the best piece of architecture in France," was the source for the porch he designed for Saint Bartholomew's Church in New York.

Medallion by Saint-Gaudens commemorating the Rhône trip
with caricatures of the three men: White at the top,
Saint-Gaudens on the left, and McKim on the right.
The Metropolitan Museum of Art, New York. Purchase,
Morris K. Jessup Fund, 1992 (1992.306).

LISIEUX. SEPTEMBER 25, 1878

MY DARLING MAMA,

Here I am, at last—off, all alone, by myself, in the land of the Goths and Vandals. So far I have got along fairly. I can understand their darned old language pretty well—but can't talk, as the small boys say, "worth a cent."

Yesterday I asked the guard at the Railway Station if I couldn't leave this—holding up my small bag—at the station. He looked puzzled and said "monsieur!" in an inquiring way, and on my repeating the question did not seem to brighten at all. Heavens, I said to myself, have I been in France for three months and—when I suddenly discovered that I was holding my circular ticket in the same hand as my bag, and the guard's attention had evidently been directed toward it. I understand almost too well at the table d'hôte. Something funny will be said and I will commence to roar, and the next minute will be immensely confused by one of the company turning around and appealing to me—and I am utterly stuck for an answer. "Cuss" irregular verbs and the feminine gender in toto, say I.

I find I can live almost as cheaply as I expected; otherwise, I should pack up for home as my treasury has already got a huge hole in it. I am working like a beaver to make up for lost time—my only enemies being rain and cold hands. I have no leisure to get blue or lonely in, absolutely no time to study French, and find I am really too tired in the evening to write letters or do anything but go to sleep. I have bought a circular for the trip I am on, which is almost as cheap as third class. I find it very comfortable, as I mostly travel on way-trains, which are resorted to by the peasantry and soldiers, who always travel third class; so very often I am alone.

Lisieux is a lovely old town, full of ancient houses and villainous boys, who plague the life out of me when I am sketching. The hotels here are a seventh heaven compared to those in the Midi and Brittany.

Bye bye, good night, love to all—and tell Dick I got his letter. You will see McKim, I suppose, about the same time you get this. He will bring you a little paper cutter, which I got for you as a souvenir of the "Hexposition." There is some chocolate also for you when the box gets through the custom house.

Ever lovingly, Stan

Bernay, September 23, 1878

Church at La Bonneville, September 22, 1878

FLERS. OCTOBER 10, 1878

MY DARLING MAMA,

What queer things time and space are; they float sometimes across the remembrance of home like clouds across the face of the sun. One thought and they are obliterated, and I am sitting again with you all, in my old seat, bearing Uncle Graham's lectures with outward serenity and inward rage. You must not think I write you when I should not; I only protested so much, because I thought you might think me an undutiful son, and sometimes, I must confess, to quiet my somewhat pricking conscience.

You can tell Uncle Graham, by the way, that I am going to write him sometime a long letter about the external, internal, political, and financial economy of France as compared with America, which he must answer at his peril. Give him my love, and Papa also, and tell him he must write me. You see this is not a long letter—it will not even cover the next page. I have written Aunt Laura and Alice to explain my non-appearance at St. Severin.

I am well and happy; the weather I am afraid is beginning to be bad. I got your letter, no. 11, wasn't it, and Dick's all right. Thank him for it, and tell him the best remedy for a sore t———- he devil—no matter, I mean, good night.

Ever lovingly thy son,
[Signed with caricature]

ROUEN. OCTOBER 17, 1878

MY DEAR PAPA,

Your letter and four others I found at the *Poste Restante* on my arrival here today.

It troubled me not a little, but I cannot allow myself to get blue—alone as I am—and so hope for the best, and that matters will come out all right in the end. Do not worry about me—please do not in any way. As soon as my money gives out I shall come home, and be very, very glad to get there.

Dick writes me that you were not feeling so well, but from what he said I suppose it was nothing serious. Do be careful. I hope it is all passed by the time this reaches you. I shall be sorry to miss Uncle Graham when I come home—and it will be queer not to send to the old number—"enfin," no more of that, as Pat said to the waiter as he filled his finger-bowl for the third time. Life after all is but a queer complexity of dreams and unpleasant realities; happy is he who can take fate calmly and quietly. "A quiet life is better than a crown"; sometimes, I think, even better than the study of architecture in foreign parts. Still I doubt if you can call it rushing about here—you can't excite the trains into more than four and a half miles an hour.

The hotels are quite fair in Normandy, clean and no bugs. The living is always passable—far ahead of anything we have in any but the largest cities. As you go up stairs you see a huge arrow—which you wonder at until you are confronted by a door on which there is the following sign: I C I. Your nose, if not your reasoning informs you it is the W.C.

I am entirely in good health and spirits. In the hope that everything will turn out rightly at home, and that you are well again.

Ever lovingly, Stan

STANFORD WHITE

rising from their seats. Of course, I said it was nothing, and laughed; but she came around and almost put her arm around my neck, while she polished off my cheek with her dishcloth—then as she turned she took my neighbor such a welch on the side of the head with it, that he must have remembered it for some time afterward.

Pretty soon the loudest of the women said she'd "had enough" and went to the end of the room to arrange her toilet in front of the glass. As she bent down, the man at the head of the table stole silently down with a syphon of *eau de seltzer*, and syringed some of it down her back. In the war of words that followed, yours truly made his escape, took his candle, and went off to bed. Then, remembering his cold, came downstairs again to find the landlord. *"Monsieur?"* *"Veuillez m'indiquer une pharmacie,"* I repeated. He took me confidentially into a corner by the elbow. *"Une femme?"* *"Non, mon Dieu, non—un medecin, une pharmacie,"* I said in despair. *"Aaaaaaah. oui, oui, oui, oui, un pharmacien.* I will show you one"—which he did, and I returned with some French "sure pop" on colds, and again went to my room. Here, having no circular ticket, I began laying my plans, and soon getting tired, began to undress. Suddenly "there was a sound of revelry by night," the band began to play, and the ball, which I had forgotten, was opened.

I won't spin it out—but Hans Breitman danced uproariously with Matilda Yane till 3 o'clock in the morning; then there was a row—I don't know what—and I think I went to sleep. There was some compensation for all this in my bill being only five francs and indeed, now I have been through it, I wouldn't have missed it for anything.

I revenged myself by going to a small hotel at Amiens, and had to pay twenty-five francs for the operation—which was quite cutting off my nose to spite my face.

My cold is better.

Love to all, Stan

NOTE

Hans Breitman and Matilda Yane were characters in a comical poem by C.G. Leland. It became a family favorite, and Lawrence Grant White used to recite it to his children.

House in Amiens

BRUGES. NOVEMBER 6, 1878

MY DEAREST MOTHER,

You are in my thoughts constantly—naturally of course—but then my buttons are coming off, my button-holes are all giving in, my heels and toes are coming through my stockings, and I have tored my rubber overcoat and I don't know how to go about to sew it up. I can get the chamber-maid to do it, but then, it is too expensive an operation. I hope you do not object to getting pencil letters—I do. I hate them, and I know a feller who always deliberately tears up his wife's letters whenever they come to him in pencil.

It seems funny to think—and I sometimes do think of it—of you all, probably eating breakfast, while I am pottering around some decayed town hall—as, for instance, in this whilom mighty city of Bruges—mighty once, somewhat melancholy now, perhaps when you think of its former grandeur: how its canals were choked with vessels from Venice, Spain, and England, and the Burghers' wives were so gorgeously attired, as to excite the envy of the Queen of France; how, as far back as five hundred years ago, it had two hundred thousand inhabitants and over—and now it has but forty-six thousand, a quarter of which, at least, are paupers.

All these things I think of now that I am in my room and have nothing else to do but ruminate, or go to bed. But I can tell you, in the day time, your whole thought is how you can hop around and see what there is to see, compress what should be a week's work into two or three days, pack your bag, and catch the midday train for Ghent tomorrow. It will be like pulling a tooth to leave this city half-digested, as I shall have to. The architecture and the old town are enough to set you wild; but when you add to these, the pictures—all there is to do is to gasp for breath, and die quietly. Here Hans Memling and his school plied their handicraft, and in one hospital alone—besides the shrine of St. Ursula—there is a whole room crammed with pictures by him and them. Full of lovely faces, simple and quiet, and all modelled up in beautiful flesh tints without a shadow; hair that seems to blow in the wind, and green and embroidered gowns that make the nails grow out of the end of your fingers with pleasure. To think that they have so many, and we have none; and that at Douai—a wretched little French town—there should be a portrait by Paul Veronese that nearly squooze tears out of my eyes, to think that so lovely a thing could be done, and I could not do it. And above all, Raphael's wax head at Lille—the loveliest face ever conceived by man. Architecture seems like poor stuff compared with things like these; and yet, when I go back to Paris and see the acres of bad painting there, I shall be very glad that I am an architect and not a painter.

(GHENT, THURSDAY)

The weather has been atrocious ever since I left Paris. I have hardly drawn a line. Rain all the time, absolutely, and when it does clear by mistake, it clears off nice and cold so I can't even hold my pencil. My cold I have at last entirely shaken off, but it was tough work.

I expect however to have a constant cold in the head if this sort of "mauvais temps" continues. Ghent is not a tenth as interesting as Bruges, and I shall clear off, I think, for Antwerp tomorrow. The Adoration of the Immaculate Lamb, by John and Hubert Van Eyk, however, is well worth, alone, a visit

"The only two old figures left on the town hall in Bruges"

Farm in Normandy

to Belgium—even to Europe. The colors are perfectly astounding, and the figure of the Virgin almost beautiful enough to be Italian.

Your letters I do not get until three or four days after they arrive, while I am away from France.

My first Belgian souper was composed of the following dishes:

1st. course:	Boiled beef and boiled potatoes.	
2nd. course:	Boiled mutton and boiled potatoes.	
3rd. course:	Boiled goose and boiled apples.	
4th. course:	Boiled cabbage.	
	Pie	
Finis:	Rotten cheese and Dutch cabbage.	

Here is a poem I have just composed on Bruges, for want of something better to do:

In Bruges, a town of towers and spires,
and streets well lined with beggars and liars,
and cats and dogs, and crooked gables,
I counted, — well, I am not able
To say how many, but should think
At least four hundred and forty stinks,
All well commingled, and all belonging
To a pack of boys. While I was drawing
They gathered around me,
and would not budge, —
Ye Gods that made them! I do not grudge
That they exist: yet if it must be,
Wash them first, so they come near me.

Here, this is too thin; I thought all this poetry was going to finish up to the bottom of the page. Good night, love to all and to thee, my darling mother, love and good night.

[Signed with caricature]

NOYON. NOVEMBER 14, 1878

MY DARLING MAMA,

This is my last sheet of note paper, which I take to tell you I am here and happy at getting a letter today from you (no. 14) and Dick. My dear mama, have I not exhorted you not to let two mails go by without letting me hear from home. Your last of Oct. 16th (and no number) I got at Boulogne on the 28th of October; and this one, just now, dated the 29th, today. You wrote 13 days apart and I got them 16 days apart. I am sure I have kept steady to the wind—but with me it would not make any difference, for if you did not get a letter for a couple of weeks or even three, all you need imagine was that I was working too hard or having too good a time, or had got entangled with a pretty girl.

But as you are three to one (and especially now) if I don't get any letter, I imagine all manner of things. Besides, setting aside sentimental reasons it is sometimes not at all convenient, as for instance this last time. I wrote my bankers to forward my letters to Ghent. I found Ghent a very uninteresting place, but danced attendance a whole day there beyond the time I cared to stay, waiting for my mail which never came. I then prepared a careful list of dates and places and gave it to the Post Office and fed the man two francs to forward anything to me, should it come; and so have been rushing to every post office (and no easy things they are to find, sometimes) till I found the next mail at this. Now you and Dick, instead of writing by the same mail, could write by different ones. Anyway try and send me a letter by every Wednesday's steamer, and as many more as you can find time to write. I am always very glad to get them. I have used up most of my paper blowing—

haven't I! Never mind, I will write you a good long letter next time. You needn't trouble yourself about dogs—I am more afraid of hotel bills than a pack of wolves. I am entirely well, and it is raining—I am always well, and it is always raining. I have bid a sad farewell to Belgium, but am very glad to get back on French soil. Love to all, good night, and a thousand kisses from

[Signed with caricature]

Interior of Laon Cathedral

LAON. NOVEMBER 20, 1878

MY DARLING MAMA,

You must think me an awful ungrateful cub to pitch into you for a sin you have not committed—nevertheless you would not have had such a beautiful cartoon as you did in your last had it not happened.

The weeks fly by with frightful rapidity, and it always seems to me that I write two letters to your one, which I can assume is nothing but an hallucination.

How fortunate it is that fate permits me to return to Paris for a day or two every three or four weeks. I should die, I think, if I did not. I hug St. Gaudens like a bear every time I see him, and would his wife, if she was pretty—but she ain't—so I don't. She is

very kind, however; asks me to dinner, mends my clothes and does all manner of things. She is an animated clothes-rack, slightly deaf—a double-barrelled Yankee, and mean to that extent that no comparison will suffice. Why fate should have ordained that such a man should be harnessed to such a woman, Heaven only knows. Nevertheless, she has been very kind to me, and I ought to be ashamed of myself for saying anything against her.

Her pretty sister and her utter antipode is staying with her now; and perhaps Fate is also wise in allowing me only to stop a day when I am in Paris.

I was on the whole tickled to death with Belgium and Belgians. You get plenty of fresh water, two clean towels and sometimes even the luxury of a slop-basin—something almost unheard of in France. Except in the small towns, the cooking was excellent. Everybody talks English, and for that matter every language—and are quite ready to do all they can for you. On the other hand, the people have very little distinctive character. They shut up their churches, and you have to pay a franc to see the pictures, and it is ("comparatively") an horribly expensive hole to be in. My trip quite bust me.

I heard Patti and Nicolini in Brussels, and had to pay the frightful price of 25 francs to do it. Nevertheless, it was one of the things that had to be done, so I did it—and it really is my first extravagance since Charlie left me.

They gave the *Barber of Seville,* and she sang, beside the Shadow Dance and a waltz. She has a most wonderful voice. It goes from Heaven knows what to the skies, and is as flexible as a piece of india rubber. She can swell on a note through six bars without a quaver—swell going down the scale and

going up—take thirds and sixths and eighths and run a scale as variegated as a kaleidescope, with an accuracy that puts an instrument in the shade. She sings with feeling (sometimes) but not with taste; she doesn't even sing the music of the Barbiere (and nothing could be more suited to her voice) properly. You catch me paying 25 francs to hear her again. Nicolini's a fraud. Brussels isn't though. Brussels is a bully place—after Paris the jolliest modern city I have come across. Indeed it is quite a miniature Paris—but in no way 2nd hand. And what is more, the hotel was the most moderate of any in Belgium.

I found Antwerp almost as antiquated a place as Bruges, and fairly gorged Rubens there. 14 portraits in one old wainscoted room and 2 by VanDyk, were enough to take your breath away. In the musuem—I don't know how many pictures. Heaps of fat legs and brawny arms and blear-eyed frowsy women whose modesty is of the most fragile kind. "Fat Mrs. Rubens," says an old author irreverently of the *Assumption,* "sits as firmly and comfortably on the clouds as if in an armchair, and gazes placidly on the wondrous scene around her; nor does her aerial flight cause her the slightest ecstasy or emotion. Ought she not to be ashamed of herself, to sit there in her flimsy attire, and personate a goddess—and a virgin, too."

Both the *Raising* and *Descent from the Cross* in the Cathedral are painted with an entirely different palette, and are wonderful: you would feel like pounding the man who said that Rubens was not the greatest painter in the world.

It stops raining now every third day—which is better than one day out of twenty-one. But it is as cold as the devil, rain or no rain. I am perfectly well, and have a frightful appetite. It is dark now at half-past four so there is no excuse for my not trying to study French. I have invested in a most moral yaller novel which I am reading as fast as my dictionary will allow me to. There, now I have written you a letter which will probably take you a month to decipher. Love to all.

Ever, ever, ever,

[Signed with caricature]

NOTE

Adelina Patti (1843-1919), internationally hailed as "one of the greatest contraltos of the nineteenth century," often sang opposite Nicolini (Ernest Nicolas, 1834-1898), a French tenor. They married in 1886.

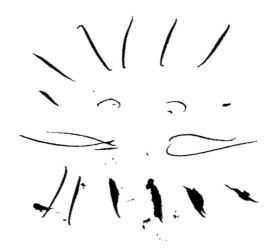

LAON. NOVEMBER 21, 1878

DEAR PAPA,

It is too bad about Dick's going off. Still, I am sure it is better for him. How things are changed, indeed! Do not write me next time that you have gone to Kamscatka, and Mama to South America, for I don't think I will come back at all then. Though we are far apart, we are still all together—and that is the main thing.

My dear Papa please do not trouble about the money—you are ever so kind. It was my intention to stay out here to August or September. This now (in any case) I am afraid cannot be. I have enough money to last me until February in Liverpool (I think). I hope to get some more from my friends.

If the worst comes to the worst, and I don't get any (which I can't think is likely) and I find I shall have to give up something which is very important to me, I may then, if it will not put you to great inconvenience, write you to send me the 500 francs. But this will be the last resort. You need the money more than I do—far. Please do not worry about me in any way; I can accept fate as it comes with perfect equanimity. If I can stay here, well and good; if not, I shall be home sooner and have less debts to pay. There is one thing however which troubles me. If I should have the good fortune to stay out here till June, my policy in the Mutual Life would have to be paid somehow or other. It is due, I think, on the 20th of June 1879, and is $48. However that is long enough ahead to let it rest.

While I was in Belgium my expenses were very heavy. This was partly caused by fees in museums and churches—averaging 4 francs a day, and hotel bills which ranged from 12 to 20 francs. I am now travelling through the very heart of France—the Île de France and Artois—and am running for the first time under my limit of 13 francs a day (sans R.R. expenses) which is very nice, especially as here you find the finest architecture in France—perhaps in the world—after the Greek.

Poor Mr. Hamill; I feel sorry for him. Still I should not feel sorry if no Mr. Stewart was out in that shameful mausoleum on Long Island.

It has given up raining, and when it doesn't snow, there is a nice thick fog. Pleasant, isn't it! Mama writes me that you are "all well again," and Dick that you "are not feeling so well." I hope Mama's account is the true one. Please take care of yourself, and don't let Mama get blue.

Ever affectionately,
[Signed with caricature]

NOTE

Alexander Turney Stewart (1803–1876), entrepreneur who created the modern department store, developed Garden City, Long Island, and amassed an enormous fortune. His wife, the former Cornelia Mitchell Clinch, was the aunt of Bessie Springs Smith, whom Stanford White married in 1884. In the controversy over his estate, Stewart's mausoleum was vandalized and his body removed and held for ransom.

Street scene, France

EUROPEAN TOUR

69

House in Tanceville

LAON. NOVEMBER 21, 1878

Why my poor little Mama, it is too bad to be deserted by both your sons. I felt thoroughly homesick for the first time when I read your letter today. Still, even if Dick does not immediately rush into a large fortune, it will do him a lot of good. If the large fortune is waiting for him, why "hurrah!" You will probably see me too—somewhat sooner than you expected. That is in fate's, and the hotel-keeper's hands.

I think I shall have to shave off my beard before I come home. This is quite an accurate portrait of me: [sketch]

I am like a revolving sun on a half shell. I wrote you a letter yesterday (fuming all the while because my mail had not come) but I am afraid I put it in too late. It is very hard to tell in these out-of-the-way places. And now you will get my letter blowing you up for not writing, probably when you are feeling blue about Dick's going away. I feel like kicking myself. I wish I felt sure of your getting as good a dinner as I do every day. It usually consists of ten courses, about as this: Soup, sometimes oysters, ragout, fish, sprouts, veal or mutton, filet or chicken and salade, fromage, dessert, nuts and raisins; and then you spend as much time as you choose, soaking biscuit in your wine and listening to the local scandal.

Travelling alone makes you very selfish. I am as careful of my personal comfort—(so long as it doesn't cost anything) as the D—l himself would be. I would get along better with my French if I had somebody to talk to. But for a few set phrases I barely open my mouth all day. I am utterly unable to enter into general conversation at the table d'hôte, and probably would be too timid, if I could.

In the ordinary run of things, I have no timidity whatever and have got to the state of laughing at people for not understanding me.

Buttons are my bête noir. How the devil can you tell which hole you are sewing through? I sew away for half an hour, and then discover—by the button coming off—that I have been sewing through the same hole all the while.

Please don't get blue and lonely—remember that I am always within ten days of home.

Ever lovingly thy son, Stan

Laon. Saturday. Nov 21st/[18]

Why my poor little Mama. It is so bad to be deserted by both your sons. I felt thoroughly home sick for the first time when I got your mail to day. Still even if Dick does not immediately rush into a large fortune, it will do him a lot of good. You will probably see him kiting back soon. Fat as a porpoise & well braced up. If the large fortune is waiting for him.. why "hurrah!!"

You will probably see me too—sooner ... you expected. ...
... & the Hotel Keeper's hands.

I think I shall have to shave off my beard before I come home. This is quite an accurate portrait of me

I am like a revolving sun on a half shell. I wrote you a letter yesterday (fuming all the while because my mail had not come) but I am afraid I put it

To his mother, Laon, November 21, 1878

To his mother, Rheims, December 1, 1878

RHEIMS. DECEMBER 1, 1878

MY DARLING MAMA,

Your last letter was the 16th, not the fifteenth as I said. The one which you wrote with the fiddles playing, and I am a bad boy to be abusing you. But you did number two of your letters No. 14, and in both of them say you had got a letter from me from Lisieux.

I am afraid the end of the world is coming! We have actually had a fine day, beginning with a starlight morning and ending with a starlight night, the sun shining gloriously, and hard frost right through the day. Just think—the first since the 21st of October. It tried to be fine today again, but finished off in a snow storm.

Do you know that I have passed into the decrepid age of 26 for nearly a month. I forgot all about it until today and—wasn't it funny—on looking back in my account book, I found that I went to hear Patti on my birthday all unbeknownst to myself.

I am now in the most historical city in France but you will probably find a much better account of it in Lippincott's Gazeteer than I can give. What interests me more than this is the seat of the Champagne trade, and I am now debating whether I can afford to get drunk on a bottle of Sillery or no. I am afraid I shall determine that I can. Now that I am writing you three times a week, you must be satisfied with short letters. Bye bye, love to Papa, a thousand kisses and good night

[Signed with a sketch]

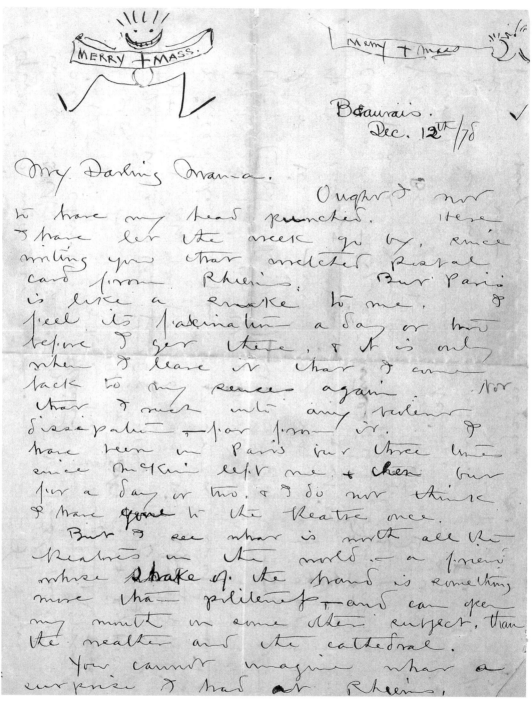

MERRY ✝ MASS.

Merry ✝ Mass

Beauvais.
Dec. 12th/78

My Darling Mama.

Ought I not
to have my head punched. Here
I have let the week go by, since
writing you that wretched postal
card from Rheims. But Paris
is like a snake to me, I
feel its fascination a day or two
before I get there, & it is only
when I leave it that I come
back to my senses again. Not
that I rush into any violent
dissipation,—far from it. I
have been in Paris but three times
since McKim left me, & then but
for a day or two. & I do not think
I have gone to the theatre once.

But I see what is worth all the
theatres in the world.— a friend
whose shake of the hand is something
more than politeness, and can open
my mouth on some other subject, than
the weather and the cathedral.

You cannot imagine what a
surprise I had at Rheims,

To his mother, Beauvais, December 12, 1878

STANFORD WHITE

74

BEAUVAIS. DECEMBER 12, 1878

MY DARLING MAMA

Ought I now to have my head punched. Here I have let the week go by since writing you that wretched card from Rheims. But Paris is like a snake to me. I feel its fascination a day or two before I get there. It is only when I leave it that I come back to my senses again. Not that I sink into any violent dissipation—far from it. I have been in Paris just three times since McKim left me and then but for a day or two, and I do not think I have gone to the theatre once.

But I see what is worth all the theatres in the world—a friend whose shake of the hand is something more than politeness—and can open my mouth about some other subject than the weather and the cathedral.

You cannot imagine what a surprise I had at Rheims the day after I got there. I found the sculpture in the portals so magnificent that I telephoned St. Gaudens to meet me there "to once." Imagine my astonishment on seeing him sail through the RR station with his sister-in-law.

Such a jolly time we had in our room (St. Gaudens and mine). I ordered a bottle of champagne, which she positively refused to taste. So "Gaudens" and I got drunk while she roasted apples and chestnuts in the fire. She is at the same time the most thoroughly innocent and self-possessed young lady I ever came across. Why the devil "Sacré G" didn't marry her instead of her sister is more than I can tell. She is a Boston girl, and we had a tremendous row on the subject of woman's rights, and she quietly paid me off, by darning all my socks and sewing buttons on all my shirts, in spite of my most earnest protestations.

In fact, she is a brick and what is more (as I believe I told you in another letter) is awfully pretty. You must not be frightened, though—I am not for her and I am sure she—or any other girl—is not for me.

If you imagine that I am going to pass a solemn and solitary Christmas you are greatly mistaken. I have been asked to Christmas dinner by Mrs. St. G. and expect to go under the table with St. G., Bunce, and Dr. Shift, about two o'clock in the morning. I will then spend about a week in Paris working on the Morgan monument and then (—but how!—) leave Paris for the last time—wend my way down by way of Bordeaux and Marseilles, and strike the sunny climes of Italy sometime in January.

France is a most jolly place for a polar bear to go sketching in winter, but for a human being, it is a little too heroic an employment. Phew! You have no idea how cold it is here. I freeze everytime I go to bed. (The sheets are like two marble slabs) and it requires all the determination I am capable of to get up in the morning. By the way did I give you the towns in my last trip—Paris, Criel, Amiens, Douai, Lille, (Belgium) Tournais, Courtrais, Oudenarde, Ypres, Dixmunden, Furnes, Bruges, Ghent, Alost, Brussels, Antwerp, Malines, Louvain, Liege, Huy, Namur—then—Paris, Senlis, Soissons, Laon, Rheims, Chalons, Epernay, Meaux, Paris.

I started off yesterday, with flying colors, for Fecamp in Normandy to make a colorful drawing of some work I saw there, but will have to beat an ignominious retreat as I found in the inside of Beauvais cathedral that I almost was frozen stiff—so I am going to finish up in the East of France, spend my last week in Paris and kite off to Italy as fast as I can. I have a letter from you and one from Aunt Sara

also. Why do you have headaches. You musn't. Tell Kate when I get sick I will remember her in my will. A million merry Christmasses to you and papa. Tis the first time we are apart. Let us drink each others health in the knowledge that we shall drink them together more pleasantly, a year from now.

Ever lovingly, Stan

Merry X Mass

NOTE

The Saint-Gaudens' Christmas party included the American painter William Gedney Bunce (1840–1916), and Eugenia Homer, Augusta Saint-Gaudens' sister. Bunce, who had met Saint-Gaudens in Rome in 1870, was sharing his Paris studio.

PARIS. JANUARY 12, 1879

MY DARLING MAMA,

After getting tripped up by the mail and sending you my last scratch, I resolved forthwith to commence a letter—no, I mean begin a letter—at once, and have at least four pages full by the time mail day came around again. That was five days ago, and here is the beginning. It is bad enough to have to work, but I'll be d—- if it's possible to write too. I directed fourteen envelopes the other evening, and only one so far has got any contents and when the others will ever get their mouths full, Heaven only knows.

Do you want to know how I pass my day? Here it is: At half past nine, Josephine (she is the *bonne*) knocks at my door. I forthwith cuss her, and lie in bed for a half an hour more—then dance out of bed, rush on my clothes, and tear down stairs and ring the doorbell five times, which is my private ring, and

usually startle that portion of the Gaudens family who still remain in the arms of Murphy.

Coffee, eggs, and oatmeal being swallowed, we forthwith make our way to the studio, and both set to work at our respective businesses. Then comes lunch hour. This is a very simple matter for St. Gaudens, who partakes of an unappetizing lunch packed up by his *femme*. With me it is quite an event; I go out and buy all my provisions and lunch like a *Seigneur* on 20 cents. Something in this way: Pâté de foie gras, boned chicken, or sardines, 4cts.; 2 petit pains, well toasted, 2cts.; Rhum pudding, 3cts.; un petit fromage suisse, 5cts.; and 2 apples, 3cts. and about 5cts. worth of wine. How is that for high. You could not do that in New York for five times the money.

Then we go to work again, and darkness—which comes here now at five o'clock—gives us a rest. I then sometimes take a French lesson—about once in three days—and go to dinner.

FRIDAY THE 17TH

My evenings are passed in fifty ways I will tell you about when I have more time; but here I am again, tripped up by the post, and I must e'en stop.

Got your New Years' letter a day or two ago. Please always try to write by the French or White Star steamers, as I depend on those mails and am disappointed when I get no letter. Dick must be all right as I got a letter from him, talking about his sickness and saying he was all right. Love to Papa. Bye, bye, my darling mother, and good night.

Thy loving son,

[Signed with caricature]

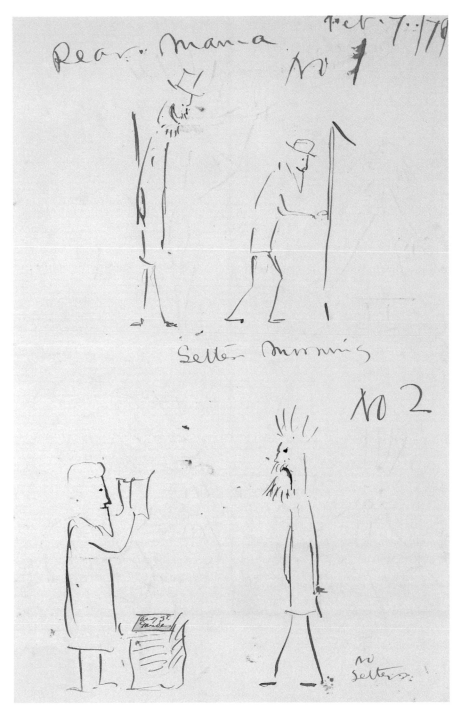

To his mother, February 7, 1879, suggesting his distress that Saint-Gaudens received more mail than he

House in France

ROME. JUNE II, 1879

MY DARLING MAMA,

Hang it all, my week passed yesterday—and I didn't write. I hate to write you postal cards, but I am afraid I shall have to be reduced to it. My time is so short here I grudge every moment; the only time I can write is of course at night, but I do not get through my dinner until eight, and then just after a bottle of wine, you don't feel like doing anything. At nine, I am ready for bed, and so the time passes. I absolutely must write a few letters to some people whom I have shamefully neglected. My dear Mama, I have not got a letter from home for fifteen days.—What does it mean?

If my time was not so overemployed, I should get blue and troubled. It is shameful the way I have not written Papa and Dick, and will do so by next mail.

The weather here is very hot, but a 7th heaven mornings and evenings. And that is just the time people tell you, you must stay in the house—Bah!

I am taking quinine, eating regularly, and carrying an overcoat to put on whenever I go into the churches and galleries, and there is about as much danger of my getting the fever as of my coming home tomorrow. Rome is a wonderful place. There are serious indications of an eruption of Vesuvius. I shall cut right down to Naples and stay a few days at Rome on my way back. Love to Papa.

Ever ever ever etc.

[Signed with caricature]

STANFORD WHITE

FLORENCE. JULY 7, 1879

DEAR PAPA,

As usual everything comes of a sudden—and I am about awakening to the fact that before you can answer this, I may be aboard steamer and on my way home.

I had hoped to be over here three or four weeks longer, but fate has willed it otherwise. I am sorry for this as I may be only able to stay two or three days in England, and I had hoped to be there some time. However I am not exactly certain how things will turn out as yet, and if I can stay on a couple of weeks or so in England, I should like very much to have a few letters of introduction, say to Leslie Stephen, Mr. Mcmillan, and any other person you think I would like to see, or might be of use to me. If you can send these, please do so at once, or they may come too late. Also write if you wish me to do anything for you in England.

I may be so short of chink that I may have to leave by a steamer from London instead of Liverpool, in which case I could not see the Gostenhofers. But in case I did go to Liverpool, do you think the Gostenhofers would expect me to pay them a visit— because if I had my passage taken, it would be very difficult to do.

I am utterly ashamed of myself for not having written you oftener, but of course you have seen all the letters I have sent home, and you could see from them how I was rushing around. I have at least a dozen kind letters from friends that I have left unanswered for three to four months. I am afraid they will never forgive me.

I will write you again soon, and only write this in a hurry, to get an answer in England if possible. Address all letters Baring Bros., London. This will have to do Mama for the weekly scrawl.

Ever lovingly your son, Stan

NOTE

Richard Grant White considered himself a "misplaced Englishman" and complained that he had been "born too far West." During the Civil War, Secretary of State W. H. Seward sent him on a tour of the great houses of Britain to prove that "there were gentlemen in the North" and dissuade the English from supporting the Confederacy. Throughout his career White corresponded with British literary figures and spent several months in London in 1876.

PARIS. AUGUST 15, 1879

MY DARLING MAMA,

Turn down my bedspread, dust out my room, tell Kate to polish up a knife and fork for me, and above all lay in a vast stock of buttons and buttonholes—for, the winds and waves permitting, you will see me within 10 days after getting this. Good Thunder, to think that my wanderings are over, and that I shall again settle down into a respectable member of society, and no longer sleep in one bed one day and another the next—the slave of guide books and R.R. Indicateurs, and the prey of Hotel-Keepers, porters, beggars, pretty girls, and the host of spiders that lay in wait for the unwary traveller; and above all, that I shall no longer go around hitching up my trousers or pinning on my collars for want of a button, but shall have a little mama who will sew them on for me and stop swearing (I do little else) at the same time.

It is too much to think of all at once. You see, this is a way of getting around that I am devilish glad to get back home again, and that I think it a "pooty" nice place after all.

You must by this time be in an awful state—not knowing whether I have sailed or haven't sailed, wondering where my telegram is, and feeling generally uncertain all around.

I sail on the "Olympus" leaving Liverpool the 23rd of August. Of course when I got to Paris there were no berths to be had for love or money. The Cunard agent however said that he could sell me a ticket on this extra steamer (which they sail on account of the great number of passengers). My chance of a stateroom when I get aboard is next to the engine, or something of that sort.

I have however written Mr. Gostenhofer, telling him that I have taken my passage on the *Olympus,* and asking if he could see that I got a good berth—or could change me if possible to the regular Cunard steamer the *Gallia,* sailing the same date. I don't know what he can do, but if he does change me to the *Gallia,* I suppose I shall have to telegraph you so.

I received Papa's and your letters all right. I suppose somebody ought to meet me at the steamer, as I am "Unacquainted" with American ways.

The steamer will probably arrive at some unearthly hour in the morning, and it would be a pity to get Papa up at that hour. Uncle Graham is fond of it—he might come. I shall get along all right in any case. I don't think I have any dutiable articles—my effects, save clothes, photographs, and plaster medallions—consisting solely of old rugs, full of holes and vermin.

Here I had hoped to have written Papa. I may drop a line again by the White Star sailing two days ahead of us.

Anyway, my dear mother, I shall see you now soon and give you a good hug—which will pay for all the bad letters in the world.

Ever lovingly, thy son,
[Signed with caricature]

PARIS. AUGUST 15, 1879

MY DARLING PAPA.

I received both your letters of introduction, etc. I shall be in London but two or three days, and so shall probably deliver none of the letters except the one to Mr. McMillan.

I hope not to have to go to him at all for money, and if I do, it will only be for five pounds or less. Will get the 'cello bridges.

I have just received news from my bankers that my trunk, which I sent 20 days ago from Florence has not yet arrived in London. It is a devil of a pickle—all my time may be taken up finding it. I sail on the extra Cunard steamer "Olympus" leaving Liverpool the 23rd of August. I could only secure my passage, and wrote Mr. Gostenhofer if he would see I got as good a berth as possible. He may be able to change me to the "Gallia" sailing same day. In which case I shall probably telegraph you. Anyway if you get no word from me I have sailed on the "Olympus" unless she happens to go down, and then I am on the "Gallia."

Do not mind about having the steamer telegraphed for and meeting me. I shall get along very well, and do not think I can have any trouble with the Custom House.

I am perfectly wild to get home, and oh! shall be so glad to see you all.

Ever lovingly thy son, Stan

I am perfectly well—couldn't be in better health, in fact—but quite thin from perspiration in Italy.

Tower in Toulouse

COLLABORATION WITH SAINT-GAUDENS

The friendship between Stanford White and Augustus Saint-Gaudens dates from 1875. As White climbed the stairs of the German Savings Bank Building, he heard a voice singing the Andante from Beethoven's Seventh Symphony. Curious, he followed the sound and discovered Saint-Gaudens in his sculpture studio. The first letters, written in 1878 after Saint-Gaudens had gone to spend a few years in Paris, show how from the outset White displayed unusual energy and devotion in the cause of his friend. Though the Senate Chamber commission never became a reality, their first cooperation on the monument to Admiral David G. Farragut was a great success. Subsequently they collaborated on the design of an elaborate funeral monument for Edwin Morgan, Governor of New York State during the Civil War, and many other projects, culminating, of course, in the *Diana* for the Madison Square Garden Tower.

Through the larger part of his stay in Paris, Stanford White made his headquarters in the Saint-Gaudens' apartment. From it, as Saint-Gaudens wrote, "White would dart off in extraordinarily vigorous excursions to the towns surrounding Paris that contain those marvels of Gothic architecture of which he was an adorer."

Back in New York White writes to announce his partnership with McKim and Mead and report on the negotiations over the Farragut monument. This collaboration reveals the extreme care the architect took to adjust and enhance the sculpture, and his endless financial maneuvering with patrons on behalf of the artist. It is also interesting to note that the aesthetic world of New York was a tight circle. The landscape architect Frederick Law Olmsted, the painter Alden Weir, Richardson, and John La Farge all could be consulted. The Farragut monument was erected in 1881 on Madison Square; the Robert Richard Randall monument was erected in 1884 in Sailor's Snug Harbor on Staten Island; the Morgan tomb was never completed because the work in process was destroyed by fire in 1883.

The majority of these letters are in the collection of Dartmouth College Library, Hanover, New Hampshire.

Sketch for a memorial

DEAR ST. GAUDENS:

Oh, most illustrious of the illustrious. I scent a big job for thee, not for me, mind you. This is but an intimation, a forerunner as it were, of what may be, not what is. Neither are you to say that you heard anything about it from yours truly.

All this 'highfalutin' means that I have just been paying a last and final visit to the abode of the Great Mogul at Brookline, and there tackled the Senate Chamber, and between us both I think we have cooked up something pretty decent. It was a very difficult problem to work out, and it suddenly struck me, as I am happy to say it struck him, that it would be a good thing to let a certain 'feller,' called St. Gaudens loose on the walls. This is no exaggeration; 'loose' is decidedly the word to use. There are about one hundred and fifty feet by twenty feet of decorative arabesque, foliage and the like, and work in panels, after the manner of St. Thomas panels. There are two marble friezes in the fireplaces, and one damn big panel for figures (Washington crossing the Delaware or cutting down a cherry tree, etc.) about forty feet by eight feet, also in colored cement, and a lot of little bits beside. The whole room is to be a piece of color, Egyptian marbles, your colored relief work and mosaic. I am absolutely sure that you will be written to about it, though of course not sure that an arrangement can be made. But, if you do get it, you will have a chance to immortalize yourself like Giotto or Michel Angelo.

I suppose Richardson will write you full particulars and that "you must give a very reasonable estimate," and that you will have a chance you will never get again, etc., etc. I should advise one thing: if any arrangement is made, that you insist, except of course in general direction, on not being interfered with by Richardson or anyone too much.

If you do the work, you will have to come home for a year or two, but with such a chance, or rather for such a chance, I should think you would go to Balahak. . . .

I will probably be in Paris about the last week in June and hope to spend at least six weeks there, I will write you beforehand and may ask you to look me up a cheap room in the fifth story of some building. You must help me to avoid being fleeced when I first get there. Indeed, I mean to test your friendship by boring you a good deal in many ways.

I do hope that you will get the Senate Chamber, and my only sorrow is that I will not be there to apprentice myself under you and learn something about decent art. Don't count your chickens before they are hatched, however.

The Dexter sketch is bully. I did not see Armstrong's medallion; sorry. I did get Michel Angelo's photograph. But I wanted yours. Here I haven't any room to write! Hell. Good-bye! Good-bye! Good-bye! I will write again soon.

Ever yours,

[Signed with monogram]

MY DEAR ST. GAUDENS:

What ragged letters I have been writing you. Three to one I believe this is. But then yours, though I confess somewhat desultory, was a royal one and paid up for a dozen of mine. Who, by the way, do you think has it now—I mean your letter? Mr. Gilder.

Mrs. Gilder heard I had a long letter from you and immediately desired my acquaintance. Complimentary, wasn't it to me? Oh! But isn't she lovely. Isn't she perfectly charming and sweet. She has given me a photograph of her baby, which I am to deliver to you in person. Had she but given me one of herself I should have been perfectly happy. You must think me a horribly mean and mercenary wretch. First to send you over $10,000 worth of work and expect you to do it for seven and then ask you to allow me a couple or one hundred dollars for doing so. In thinking over the math before I got my estimate, I got at the eight thousand allowance for you in the following way—you remember you told me you could do the four figures for $6,000 and I thought that a bas-relief with eight figures. Four in high and four in low relief could be done for somewhat near the same sum. . . .

I shouldn't wonder but that Morgan would go the nine thousand dollars provided the other sculptor estimates higher than you did—which I feel sure he will. Now, I have no doubt you are cussing and swearing all this while and saying 'Confound the man; the thing can't be done for anywhere near the sum,' etc., etc. In that case, my dear boy, all you have to do is to think up some brilliant idea that can. And as for the hundred or two dollars, let them go to hell. By the way, how long will you take to do the work? I mean finished in stone? I told Morgan eighteen months to two years. How's that, me boy?

I hope you will let me help you on the Farragut pedestal. Then I shall go down to fame even if it was bad, reviled for making a poor base to a good statue.

Did Richardson write you about the Albany matter? I am afraid it has gone to grass. I haven't seen him since. I hope you answered my last at once.

I sail on the 18th of June, unless something happens—something always does happen!

Good bye

[Signed with monogram]

NOTE

Richard Watson Gilder (1844–1909), poet, assistant editor of Scribner's Monthly *and later editor of* The Century. *La Farge, Saint-Gaudens, Whitman, White, and other artists and writers were frequent guests at his New York home, known as The Studio. White designed covers for both* Scribner's Magazine *(1887) and* The Century *(1893).*

NEW YORK. JUNE 21, 1878

DEAR ST. GAUDENS:

Yours just received this morning and I thank the Lord for getting it. I began to think you were disgusted with me, which would have been very wrong; or that you were again attacked with the fever, which would be worse; or that, which would be worst of all, you had gone to Rome, which I hope to heaven you will not do until after I have left Paris.

It is just like you to offer me a bunk. Do you think I would inflict myself upon you? We shall see. I have been working like Hell and Damnation and have just been able to finish the drawings and put them in such a state that contracts can be taken on them. They are at present estimating, and it will take a week before they are in. So you see I have had to put off my passage, and I now sail on the French steamer *Perière*, on Wednesday July 3d. Who do you think is coming with me? Even McKim. I am tickled to death. He is coming over for but a six weeks' trip but still it is perfectly jolly. We will land at Havre and take the express train for Paris and so will arrive there I suppose about the 15th or 16th. I will pay my respects on you immediately.

I have come to the conclusion, and I feel almost sure that you will too, that eight figures will be too much for the monument. So my present idea is as follows: At the front put four figures of angels, well in relief, or put a figure in between the two in relief, but on the sides and back arrange some conventional foliage or flowers. It would give it more dignity and it seems to me a centre of interest which the mere fringe of angels would not have. However, all this is your work and for you and you only to decide, and I am going to impress the same on Morgan. The above scheme would only have five figures and would give both you and the cutters less work, would it not? However, for Heaven's sake, not considering any two or three hundred dollars to me, what you want to do is to estimate on the work, giving a full and fair profit to yourself. Then if Morgan refuses to accept, let us cook up some scheme that will come within the figure. . . .

[Signed with caricature.]

TOURNAI. C. NOVEMBER 1878

DEAR ST. GAUDENS:

Something more to do? Of course! You do not think I would take the trouble to write you without some selfish reason. I hope it will not be your death, however. It is only to warn you that I am going to have my letters sent to your studio. All you will have to do is to put them aside in a nice little niche, and then, when you get word from me, forward them to some Poste Restante and charge the stamps and envelopes to me. The only reason I trouble you is because if there is a draft for a 1,000 francs in one of them I do not wish it to go stalking all over the country after me.

Is not McKim an old fraud? He has neither written me nor gone to see my mother, nor anything. Poor fellow; he must be having a hard time—and yet it is just like him.

An Englishman in the sixteenth century describes Calais in his diary as "a beggarly extorting hole, monstrous dear and sluttish." All I can do is agree with him.

And now, old boy, having been "werry" modest, the real reason I am writing you is to tell you about an acquaintance of yours. Perhaps you have seen her, and I am wasting my time and making a fool of

myself; nevertheless, here goes: I was at Lille yesterday and went to the museum. I suppose it is the best provincial collection anywhere; but I wandered past pen and wash drawings by Michel Angelo and Raphael, by Fra Bartholemew, by Tintorretto, Francia, Signorelli, Perugino, Massaccio, Girlandajo, pen and wash drawings by Verrocchio and one even by Donattelo, even drawings by these men, and ink and wash drawings at that. I wandered past them with a listless sort of air. I was on a hunt for something else, even a wax head by Raphael. I couldn't find it and was about to appeal to the guardian, when suddenly, 'Holy Moses! Gin and seltzer!' everything, anything, would be but as straws in the whirlpool.

When you have made up your mind that a thing should look one way, and it looks another, you are very apt to be disappointed. For a minute I gasped for breath; the next, like a vessel changing tack, my sails shook in the wind and I said, 'Is this thing right?' And then the utter loveliness of it swept all other feelings aside. Do you know that it is colored, and that all it needs is eyelashes to be what people call a "wax figure," that the skin is flesh-color, the lips red, the eyes chestnut, the hair auburn, the dress blue and the pedestal gold? It is easy enough to take exception to all this; and your reason will immediately tell you it is wrong. But then you go and look at it, and wish you may die or something, you no more question it not being 'high art' than you think of a yellow harvest moon being nothing but a mass of extinct volcanoes.

It is no use going on; I shall have to wait until I can dance around your studio to express my enthusiasm. Get down on your knees in front of your auto-type which gives but a half idea of it. Never was so sweet a face made by man in this world; and I am sure if they are all as lovely in the next it must be heaven indeed.

I have got a bully idea for you, too. Right alongside was a little medallion in wax, colored, of Savonarola, perfectly stunning, no bigger than your little medallions. I am sure you could do something with it.

I am now in Belgium, the landscape is highly interesting, something like this [sketch]

I have swallowed the whole bottle of your damned red syrup (Auberge?) or what ever you call it with little efffect.

[Signed with caricature.]

NOTE

The bust of a woman White describes has an intriguing history. Bequeathed to the Lille Musuem in 1834 the sculpture became the most popular piece in the collection with visitors flocking to see it. As the museum guidebook explains, "At the time of its glory, there were many theories about its creation. Wicar [the donor] believed it was from the time of Raphael. From there it was only a step to attribute it to the master. Then they dreamed of Leonardo." Eventually the sculpture was attributed to the Flemish artist François Duquesnoy, on the basis of its close relationship to his other busts, particularly his portrait of Saint Suzanne.

SEPTEMBER 6, 1879

H'on board the Olympus.

I did not answer your question about the height of the figure. I ought to have my nose flattened. But I wasn't a responsible being, so 'nuff said.' My feeling would be to lower it 'by all means.' I think the figure would be in better proportion to the pedestal, too. But that is a matter for you to decide, and you can settle it very easily by having Louis make a Farragut eight feet two in paper and seeing the effect. With the paper pedestal already made, that would be near enough to judge.

One reason I did not answer the question was because I thought I would wait until I could see the Lafayette in Union Square and send you the measure. I don't care a damn about the Lafayette myself, but I will measure it immediately on my arrival and write you what it is. There is nothing else I can think of that I should write you about before I get home.

Heigh-ho! This is the dullest business I ever came across. There is no amusement, nobody to talk to, and I am so dead of ennui that I can't even read, much less write or draw. Did I ever say I liked the sea? I'm a fried pumpkin blossom if I ever say so again; and if I ever go aboard a Cunarder more, much less an extra one, I'll be damned into the end-most corner of the last circle of the worst hell that any poet, ancient or modern, has ever created or chooses to create. And then the eleven old maids! Oh, Lord! I started timidly making a drawing the other day, and in five minutes I had them all literally about my ears, with "Oh, how nice!" "What are you drawing?" "Do let me see it"; "Now I think it's real mean"; "Well, can we see it when you get through?" etc., etc., one of them actually leaning on my shoulder. Ugh! Commit me to America for ill-breeding and curiosity! Boarding-house Yankees!!! What more awful creatures exist on the face of the earth? Let us change them for something more pleasant, and hop like Byron's Don Juan from the ridiculous to the sublime.

Do not fail to spend at least a week in London before you come back. There are oceans of things there, far more than in Paris or indeed any place that I have come across—Greek and Renaissance coins and medallions by the hundred: and my hair alternately stood up and flattened down in front of the Greek and Assyrian bas-reliefs. If I could only have got casts of some of them, I should have been a happy man for life. Then again in the South Kensington Museum, besides casts of everything that ever was or ever will be there are at least forty to fifty screaming Renaissance panels: for instance, the one you have and I bought in Florence is one of them, originals, and lots of portraits by Della Robbia, Civitella and all manner of things. I did not see half. I never saw such a country as England. Do you know that at Windsor Castle there are upwards of one hundred drawings of Holbein's like those I copied at Basle? D'ye understand 100!!!—some of them even more splendid—and forty oil paintings. And to think I did not go there? Oh! Oh! Sorrow the day that I was born!

We steamed out of Queenstown at ten knots an hour, into rather nasty weather which kept by us for five days, ending up in a roaring old storm, the night of which we succeeded in making the enormous sum of two knots an hour, wind dead ahead. The first day out the wind blew very hard, and the majority of the ladies thought we were going to the bottom. I said to the little third officer, "Nice sea on."

"Yes sir."

"Still, sailors don't mind anything like this."

"Oh, no, sir. It isn't more'n a half gale."

Monday it was a little stronger.

"Yes, sir, pretty fresh this morning."

Tuesday it blew like hell.

"You wouldn't call it a storm, though, would you?" I said.

"Oh, well, sir, no sir, it's hardly a storm, but it's pretty dirty."

Wednesday the ship began trying to get her stern over her nose. There were six at table, including the Captain, Purser, Doctor and myself. About eleven o'clock at night I managed to get on deck. The sea was pretty wild, but I thought in a good smacking storm that the waves would be bigger than the ship; as it was, there were two or three to the length of the vessel. So I staggered up to the little officer with whom I had got quite friendly.

"Well, what do you think of this?"

"Oh, sir, I guess they won't sleep much to-night."

"Still," said I, coming back to my oft repeated question. "You wouldn't call this a very heavy sea, would you?"

"Why, good heavens, sir! What would you like? I think you would like to sink the ship!"

We had a high old time that night; the steerage hatchway was stove in, and the front staircases to the hurricane deck carried away, and the doctor got a huge wave into his cabin and has been on his back with lumbago ever since. Meanwhile, the ship had been getting so stuffy, with everything battened down, that we all thanked God when her nose was sailing clear of the wave and we could breathe fresh air again.

I am only writing this to fill up time; and, if it is as damned stupid work reading as it is writing it, I'm sorry for you. Here is a corrected inventory of the ship's company. The eleven old maids have been reduced to seven; there are three widows who ought to be old maids; one widow who is pretty and correspondingly naughty; a thing that calls itself a she-doctor and rejoices in being the sister of Vic Woodhull, and Miss Lou Claflin, a girl whom nobody knows anything about, who keeps entirely to herself and is consequently looked down upon by all the old maids; the pretty little girl who has turned out the most interesting of the passengers; Mr. Wright, her father, ex-Mayor of Springfield, and his partner, Mr. Covell, a New York lawyer; a humble Western man and his little boy, and an Irish priest.

Thus far did I get and no further—various things and laziness interfering. We got to Fire Island at six, Friday night, and quarantine at eight o'clock and had to lay there all night.

Don't read this until you have nothing to do.

NOTE

Louis Saint-Gaudens (1854-1913), sculptor and assistant to his brother.

Victoria Woodhull and Tennessee Claflin were sisters noted for their beauty and wildly eccentric behavior. A clairvoyant, a feminist, and the publisher of Woodhull and Claflin's Weekly, *Victoria was the first woman candidate for President of the United States in 1872.*

MY BELOVED SNOOKS:

I have but a moment to write and do so in the utmost haste to let you know the following fact.

I made yesterday three unsuccessful attempts to measure the Lafayette and get in the lock-up. Today I came near succeeding in both. Here is the result. It is impossible to get an accurate measure without a step-ladder and a requisition on the city government! But I will swear that it is not over eight feet five or under eight feet three. If it had not come so near to our figure, I should have telegraphed you. If you still stick to eight feet six I do not think you will go much wrong. But I myself should most certainly advise reducing the figure and base to eight feet six (i.e. figure 8'2" or 8'2 ½" or even 8'3" whatever would make an even equation with your 65 inches and base 4 inches).

I think it would look best any way and the Lafayette is full 9 ½ in the air—(and yet to balance that somewhat we have our more bulky base).

Write me at once what you have decided to do. . . .

MY DEAR GAUDENS:

You can form no idea of what a fearful state of drive I am in. I have been home but eight days. I have had to spend four of them out of town, and with McKim's business, as well as mine and yours pressing on all sides. I have seemed to have done nothing but rush, rush around after people with little or no result. Things do seem to crop up like hydras' heads all around me. I had a long talk with Richardson and Olmsted about the Farragut pedestal. They both seemed to like it very much, Richardson especially, and both liked it better than the old one. Olmsted said he felt very sure you could have any site you might choose. He still favored the one in front of the Worth Monument, and did not at all like the one we think of in Madison Square. He thought it a sort of shiftless place, which would give the statue no prominence whatever. He seemed to think it might be anywhere along the sidewalk, as well as the place we proposed. He suggested the following places: in the triangles formed by the intersection of Broadway and Sixth Avenue, in which way the whole of the little parks would be made to conform to the pedestal, or at a place somewhere near the entrance of the Central Park. He also suggested just north of the fountain in Union Square.

STANFORD WHITE

I myself still favor the Madison Square site, its very quietness being a recommendation. Of the other sites, the one north of the fountain in Union Square seemed far the best.

The elevated railway, it seems to me, knocks the others. We could not take a place directly opposite the Fifth Avenue Hotel; we could, of course, but just above it is by far the best place.

I have not seen La Farge about the pedestal, or Babb, on whose judgment I mostly rely. La Farge is not coming abroad, and his affair he wrote me about is all glass bubbles. He asked most kindly after you. He has gone most extensively into stained glass, making all kinds of experiments. Some of his work impressed me as much as ever, but his decoration and figure drawing looked pretty sloppy, after the old work.

About Morgan's monument, I have both good and bad news to communicate. His son has died and Mead says he is in a most howling hurry for his monument. I have not seen him yet, as I believe he is not in town, nor have I been able to completely understand Casoni and Isola's failure and must see them first before I can see him. But it does not complicate us in any way; and but for this unhappy affair of Morgan's son dying, I might have managed things so it would have been better for you. I may do it yet

and shall try all my might, but of course I can tell nothing until I see him.

I got your note about the little photograph of the Farragut and shall see about it at once. You must not get mad if I do not do things as quickly as you might think I ought to. I have had my nose jammed immediately to the grindstone in the office, and you will have to make allowance for it.

I have just been up to see my aunt in Newburgh, and I am writing this in the boat on my way to New York.

I drove up to Armstrong's and saw him for a little while. He said he had just got a note from you. He was pleasant as ever, but he seemed to me a much more saddened man than when he was in Paris. They have either had some pecuniary misfortune, or the lonely life up there is telling on him. He spends half his time farming, and he told me I was the first artist he had seen for three months. He asked me all manner of questions about you and your work. He has done very little painting since he has been home.

NOTE

George Fletcher Babb (1836–1915), architect and close friend of White, McKim, and Saint-Gaudens. He remodeled the Saint-Gaudens studio in Cornish, New Hampshire.

57 BROADWAY, NEW YORK
SEPTEMBER 1879
MR. HORGUSTUS GAUDENS
NO ARTIST PARIS

. . . I feel quite sot up. Babb likes the new pedestal better nor the old one, and likes it very much; and he thinks that eight feet three to eight feet five a very good size for the statue; but he said he wouldn't make it smaller. I am goin to see Morgan tomorrow, and tremble in my boots now.

I've got my trunk! I've got my peacock's skin, and had to pay 5 5 5 5, four little gold pieces, for the pleasure. But I've got 'em and the next time they go on a railway travel I'll eat trunk, peacock's feathers and the railroad officials in the bargain—Will go to see about the photograph of Farragut tomorrow. I send you the letter I started on the Olympus. I don't know why I send it. It isn't worth the stamp. I had a frightful row with the Woodhull woman, and I think she hid the book it was written in. They found it some time after the boat was in port stuffed behind one of the cushions.

There is nothing about conventionalization of the sea, is there? The sea was altogether too much for me to draw, but I may write you a little about it. As to conventionalization, by reason of place and material, I believe it is necessary the more I think of it; and I think you believe so, too, even though you won't ackowledge it. Also I am sure that whatever you do yourself will be bully and much better than if anybody else meddled with it.

Everybody sends love and everybody wishes you home—I send love to everybody and wish you home none the less.

Lovingly.

[Signed with caricature]

57 BROADWAY, NEW YORK
OCTOBER 15, 1879
DEAR [SAINT-GAUDENS CARICATURE],

Some time ago I took the two pedestals to La Farge. His criticism was very quick and to the point. He liked them both; but liked the first sketch the best, for the reason that he thought it simpler and more of a whole, and that of two designs he liked the one that could fall back on precedent, rather than the more original one, unless the original one was so astonishingly good that it compensated for its strangeness.

Funny, coming from La Farge, wasn't it?

I then asked him to sail into the last pedestal and tell us what to do and how to better it.

He said the curving, or rising, of the line upward from the ends toward the pedestal proper was an insuperable objection. He disliked it any way, and gave as his chief reason that it was antagonistic with the circular plan of the seat and destroyed the perspective almost entirely.

He liked the decorative treatment very much and the dolphins very much.

OCT. 21

Now the only thing that troubles me about his criticism is his objection to the curved rising line of the back of the seat, for the reason that it bothered me considerably and had lain on my conscience like flannel cakes in Summer. I am sure it will not look well, and I am almost equally sure that a straight back, or one very slightly and subtly rising will. Almost everybody (architects) have spoken about it.

Still, if you feel very strongly about it, why let us keep it. I send you some tracings with this and you can see what I mean.

Sketch for Saint Gaudens's statue of Deacon Samuel Chapin, Springfield, Massachusetts

As you have lowered your figure three inches, we might lower the pedestal by that amount, raise the ends of the wall three inches, and lower it three inches where it joins the pedestal. Then the bulk would be very little more than the present design, and I do not see how it could injure your figure. Of course, I should know about this as soon as possible, as I have to know it before I send you the full size outlines of the pedestal and back. If you think it necessary, you can telegraph, but it will only gain ten days.

Also, you clay-daubing wretch, why did not you tell me which site you wished. You wrote me that you thought them all "good."

I myself strongly like the Madison Square site and 'so do we all of us,' but you must decide, and for God's sake do so and then hire a hall forever afterward.

I wonder if there will be any St. Gaudens left after reading all these letters.

Poor boy.

[Signed with caricature]

MY DEAR OLD BOY:

Here is the long-promised epistle. I shall try and not make it more than forty-eleven pages long nor must you think I have been put to too much trouble. I am just as interested in the success of the pedestal as you are; nor, alas! shall I see many such chances in my life to do work in so entirely an artistic spirit, unhampered by the—well—small hells that encircle us on every side; women who want closets, for instance.

I arrived in New York on Saturday the 6th of September and went to the office on Monday the 8th. For the first week I had my hands and my head as full as I ever wish them to be of things to do and think over. I wrote you a letter at the end of it coming down the Hudson on the Powell. That brings us to Monday the 15th. On the 17th, I think, I wrote to Fordyce & Browning, the contractors who gave the bid on the old pedestal, to call at the office and give me a bid on the revised design. Mr. Fordyce called the next day and took the drawings away with him but did not bring his estimate in until six days after! I had seen Olmsted meanwhile and written you about the site; but I did not think it advisable to see Cisco or send your letter to the park commissioners until I had a definite bid on the pedestal. Meanwhile I had begun to be pretty worried and scared, for both prices and labor had gone up nearly twenty-five per cent, and I was not at all surprised when Mr. Fordyce told me the lowest bid he could make on the pedestal was two thousand seven hundred dollars. We went all over the plans carefully but could see no way of cutting it down. So I sat down, said 'hell and damn it!' and then made up my mind that if we died we would die hard. So I sent Cisco your letter and one from myself, asking for an

appointment, drank a brandy cocktail, and told Fordyce if he couldn't devise some way of reducing the bid, never to darken the door of McKim, Mead & White's office again. Next morning I got a letter from Cisco saying he would be in Saturday the "hull" day long; and Fordyce appears with a sort of a yaller green bluestone in his hand, which he says is the "grandest," (he is a Scotchman), stone on the market, and that he will build the pedestal for three hundred and fifty dollars cheaper. He swore it was as strong as the bluestone, and to prove it picked up a piece of bluestone and hit them together and smashed his own stone into a thousand splinters. Convincing, wasn't it?

Nevertheless, the stone turned out to be a very good stone and a very stunning color. I'll send you a specimen of it.

So Saturday noon I sailed down to Cisco's office, with the photographs in one hand and my stone in the other. He received me kindly, read over your letter again and asked me what he could do for me. I told him how long we had worked on the pedestal and how anxious we were to have it built, how the bids had come over the amount in hand, and how we hoped for the Committee's assistance. He said, 'Ah! Dear me!' two or three times; thought pedestal No. 1 would be very grand, and liked pedestal No. 2 almost as well, liked the stone, too. And at the end he rose from his seat and said he was very sorry that General Dix was not alive, that he would have been the proper person to apply to, that as for himself he really could do nothing about it, that the two thousand dollars would always be at my disposal, and then wished me good morning.

"Then you do not think that any more money could be raised?" I said as I shook hands with him.

"Possibly—possibly," he replied. "You had better see Gov. Morgan, as he is Mr. St. Gaudens' friend."

I went away quite discouraged. The Committee is evidently utterly disorganized and without a head, and what disheartened me most was Cisco's apparent utter lack of interest in the whole matter. I then wrote him three notes in succession about a mile long and very wisely tore them all up and boiled them down to the four-page letter which I send you. After seeing Cisco, I had spoken to my father and asked his advice. Cisco, by the way, at first supposed I was the man who was going to contract for the pedestal. So my dad told me he would give me a formal letter of introduction to him which would make him at least listen courteously to what I had to say again. What he did write was a letter of about a dozen lines, expressing our cause strongly and putting the point to Cisco in a way worthy my four pages twice over. The plan I had formed was to get the list of subscribers and then make attacks on all of them, with my dad's assistance, until I came across some feller who took enough interest in the thing to make the cause his own. I sent my dad's letter and my own to Cisco in the same envelope and was asked to call on him next day.

He was as kind as before, told me he had computed the interest and found there was two thousand four hundred and fifty dollars, just the sum we want to build the plain shell, above the nine thousand dollars. He said it would be next to impossible to get a list of the subscribers and that it would be very foolish for me to try to do anything about raising any more money now, especially as the statue was behindhand, but that, when the statue and pedestal were put up, if they were a success, he thought there would be no doubt but that the extra six hundred dollars or so

could be raised among a dozen or so of the subscribers. For instance, he would give fifty dollars, perhaps Morgan one hundred and so on. He then bade me 'good morning' and told me to see Morgan and get his advice.

So I marched off with joy in my soul and had hard work to stop myself writing you a high-cockalorum of a letter at once. I did not write you before for the reason that so far nothing was settled, and I saw no reason of disheartening you when possibly matters might turn out for the best; and, after seeing Cisco, I thought it safest to see Morgan, rather than write you a paen of victory and have to take it all back by next post.

Alas, I only did too wisely, or rather I won't say alas. Who the devil cares for Morgan? I saw him three times after this, but on each occasion he was in a bad humor, and I did not venture upon the pedestal. Last week I called to see him, called again about his old mausoleum, and took the photographs of the pedestal with me in case the opportunity was favorable. He did not want to see me about his monument, although he had told me to call, but asked what I had in my hands. I thought I had better settle matters at once, and I showed him the pedestal and told him as quietly as I could how we stood and what Cisco had said.

He immediately got up on a high horse and acted in a most outrageous manner, misunderstood everything I said and in fact would listen to nothing. "The Committee wouldn't guarantee a cent." "Mr. St. Gaudens had a contract and he should stick to it." "The idea of asking for more money." "The Committee wouldn't pay a cent, nor would they go begging." "Cisco could speak for himself." "Let him stick to his contract," etc., etc., etc. And he finished

up by raising his hand and calling on his secretary to witness that he wouldn't give a cent, not one God-damn cent. Then he said he didn't want to talk any more about it, so I picked up my hat and walked out of his office, with my fingers itching to clutch him by the throat.

His whole manner of acting was as if we were trying to come some game over the Committee and that he brushed us away as beneath listening to. I was boiling mad and at first a little troubled what to do, and wisely slept over it. The next morning I wrote him the letter enclosed and went immediately down to see Cisco, told him what had happened and showed him the letter I had sent to the Governor. He metaphorically patted me on the back, told me not to mind Morgan; that this is entre nous, his physicians had told him that he could not live more than two or three years and that in consequence he was in a constantly depressed and morbid condition.

So I went away again highly elated, as I was afraid Cisco would say, "Well, you had better drop the whole matter and do what the contract calls for." He at least is our friend, and I am sure will gather others to us. This was four days ago.

Now you know all about it: what has happened and exactly how the matter stands. You must draw your own inferences and tell me what to do. There will be above the contract for the pedestal about six hundred to seven hundred dollars extra for the cutting of the reliefs. Toward this, at a pinch, the difference in the cost of casting a figure eight feet three instead of nine feet might legitimately go, and I feel almost sure that the balance can be raised among the subscribers when the time comes; but of course it is a risky thing, and one that you must decide for yourself.

I have told you everything and at frightful length; and now the pack is on your shoulders, and you can throw it off which way you choose. You're boss, and I await your orders. If you so decide, we have plenty of time to design a new "chaste and inexpensive" pedestal.

If, however, you decide, as I think you will, to go on with our last design, write me so at once. I found out from the contractors that they could cut the stone in the winter and put up the whole pedestal, foundation and all, within three weeks in the Spring. So we are not more than moderately pressed in that regard, but it is important that you should start immediately on your work modelling the reliefs, etc. Therefore, if you choose, you can telegraph simply "Stanford, New York." I will leave word to have any telegram so addressed sent to the office, and I will understand that you mean go ahead and will contract for the pedestal at once.

Assez! Assez! c'est fini.

Look up! Hire a hall! I have spent two evenings writing this and hope it will go by this week's White Star steamer.

For you that have to read it and the "wealth of correspondence accompanying it"—all I can say is 'God pity you and be with you, old boy, forever.'

[Signed with monogram]

October 20th

NOTE

John Jay Cisco (1806–1884), financier and politician, who rose from owning a tailor shop to be "one of the leading and most conservative of the bankers on Wall Street" according to his obituary in the New York Times; *member of the Farragut Monument Commision.*

Farragut Monument, Madison Square, New York
Photograph by David Finn

57 BROADWAY, NEW YORK
DECEMBER 17, 1879

DEAR OLD FELLOW:

. . . When I saw Cisco yesterday, he said he "did not feel authorized to sign any paper, as they had a contract with you to furnish a pedestal, and, as soon as you furnished it, they would pay you the money; but if Messrs. Fisher & Bird would call, he would assure them that it would be all right. As contractors, however, usually want something safer than assurances, and Fisher & Bird said they would feel entirely satisfied if I went your security, I forthwith did it and enclose you a copy of my engagement. As I 'ain't' got a cent, and therefore run no risk, I consider it the most magnificent exemplification of friendship 'wot' ever occurred. . . .

I wouldn't have said anything about the security but for this reason. In case, God forfend, you should happen to part company with this world, complications might arise. So just write an order; asking the treasurer of the Farragut, etc., etc., whatever it is, to pay Messrs. Fisher & Bird the total amount of money accumulated for the pedestal. Send the paper to me, and I will stick it in our safe to await contingencies.

Then also you must write me an order saying "This authorizes Mr. Stanford White to contract in my name for the pedestal of the Farragut statue." signed Augustus St. Gaudens.

I feel that I should have my tail kicked for making you wait so long for your measurements to start work on the reliefs. How the devil you are going to get through I can't see. You will, however, have been getting ahead on other things, that is some consolation.

The truth is I had the thing pretty well along when one Sunday Babb came in, damn him, and said in his usual way of springing a bombshell on you, "Well, if you take the rise out of the back of your seat, you'll get the pedestal too heavy and make the figure look thin." Then, as usual, he shut up like a clam and wouldn't say more. Now, as I care too much for Babb's opinion, and my conscience would never have forgiven me if I got the pedestal too heavy, I began floundering around trying to improve the matters until McKim came along and said, "You're a damn fool. You've got a good thing. Why don't you stick to it." So I've stuck to it.

You will see, however, what changes have been made by comparing the plans I send you and those I left with you. The plan of the pedestal has a flatter curve, and the whole pedestal is broader and lower. Babb approves, everybody approves, and I am consequently happy.

After a heavy consultation, I have kept the rise in the back of the seat in a modified and more subtle, hire a hall, form; so you'll be satisfied.

All I have to say is if any Greek temple had any more parabolic, bucolic or any other olic kind of curves about it than this has, or if the architect had to draw them out full size, a lunatic asylum or a hospital must have been an addenda to an architect's office. I hope you will not go into a hospital trying to understand them, old boy. . . .

About the models: The ones we want first, of course, are the fish and the sea and the sword, as those are in the contract. Everybody likes the fishes, so I would make them like the little model "better as you

STANFORD WHITE

can." As to the sea, do just as you damn please, and it will be sure to be bully. You must make it stormy though. As for conventionalism, fire away as you choose; our difference of opinion is only one of words.

By the way, did you ever read the description of the horse in the book of Job? "Hast thou given the horse strength? Hast thou clothed his neck with thunder? Canst thou make him afraid as a grasshopper? The glory of his nostrils is terrible. He paweth in the valley and rejoiceth in his strength."

Of course, a horse's neck is not clothed with thunder. It's all damned nonsense. But would a realistic description have gone to your guts so?

I've got to stop now or I'll drop. Loads of love to Louis and the kindest remembrances to your wife and sister-in-law. To thyself K. M. A.

[Signed with caricature]

57 BROADWAY, NEW YORK
DECEMBER 27, 1879
DEAR OLD HOSS:

This is the last I have to say about the Farragut until I hear from you. . . .

How the devil you are going to get through with all your work I can't see. Why don't you make the models for this half-size. I think you will be a damn fool if you don't get some skillful young Frenchman, who you can get cheap, to help you on the Randall. You would save money by it, I should think, by having it cast in France.

You will, of course, notice the height for your Farragut figure (the bas-reliefs) is reduced by about four inches. This is a little bad for the figures, but it

is better for the statue, and to that everything should be sacrificed. I am going to try another step out near the sidewalk and terrace up nine or ten inches, thus getting the statue as much above the eye as it is in the little clay model.

This is my idea of the arrangement. [sketch]

. . . I tell you something which will be far worse than the Fifth Avenue Hotel. That is Bartholdi's huge hand and arm which is right opposite the Worth Monument. Here is an elevation of Madison Park from Twenty-sixth Street to Twenty-third Street. Seward would be about nineteen feet high, if he stood up. Never you mind; it is not size but guts that tells. You could stick the Parthenon inside a small ring of the Grand Central Depot. Now, this is all I have or will have to say about the Farragut, unless it will be to answer something that you wish to know. I am sure you will thank the Lord for it more than I do.

NOTE

The torch arm of the Statue of Liberty was exhibited at the Centennial International Exhibition in Philadelphia in 1876 and later in Madison Square in New York as part of the fund raising effort for Bartholdi's work. Fifty cents bought a climb to the top and donations were encouraged. Eventually the arm was returned to Paris to be attached to the rest of the statue, which was erected in New York harbor in 1886.

The monument to General William G. Worth, hero of the Seminole and Mexican wars was erected between Fifth Avenue and Broadway and 25 and 26th streets in 1857.

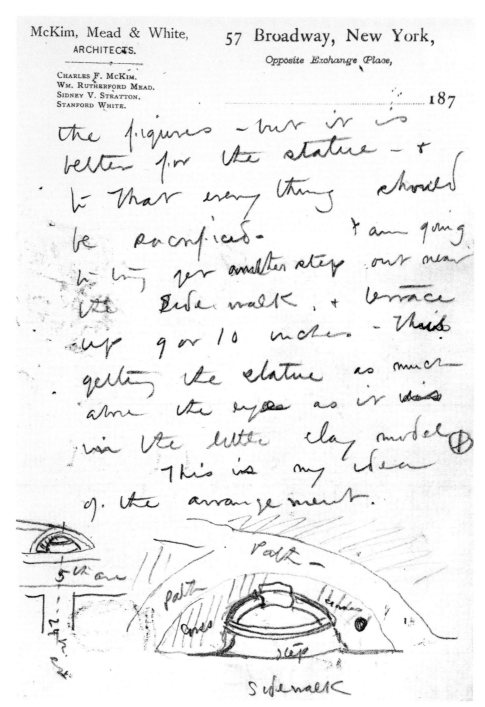

McKim, Mead & White,
ARCHITECTS.

CHARLES F. McKIM.
WM. RUTHERFORD MEAD.
SIDNEY V. STRATTON.
STANFORD WHITE.

57 Broadway, New York,

Opposite Exchange Place,

_____ 187

the figures — but it is
better for the statue — +
to that every thing should
be sacrificed — + am going
to bring yet another step out near
the sidewalk, + terrace
up 9 or 10 inches — Thus
getting the statue as much
above the eyes as it was
in the little clay model ⊕
This is my idea
of the arrangement.

To Saint-Gaudens, December 27, 1879, with sketch of the Farragut site

STANFORD WHITE

FEBRUARY 24, 1880

BELOVED:

Bis first, pummeling afterward. I suppose you are much obliged to me for the Life of Farragut. Now that you have sent the statue to the casters I send you the Life. It goes by Thursday's steamer.

There is another thing I wish to know about, namely, the inscription. I submitted a draft of about the one we decided on in Paris to my Dad, and then took it up and saw young Farragut and madame. They liked it very much and Mrs. Farragut made a few senseless and sentimental suggestions—but the trouble is my Dad did not like it at all. He said it would be a most difficult thing to do; and, thinking, until lately, that you were coming over in May, and that we would have time to settle its definite form then, I planned to invest in Farragut's Life and go over it with my dad and then let him make up something of his own which we could talk over when you appeared. I will now attend to it at once in order to be ready for any contingency. Your idea, however, is to draw it on the stone here and perhaps have Louis and an assistant cut it, is it not? Yet, what time will you have to have that done? I wish you could hurry Barbeza up. The middle of June is not a fortunate time for the unveiling, not because it is so warm, but because everybody will have gone out of town, and I am afraid it will put the members of the Committee badly out of humor. Both Cisco and young Farragut said very strongly that the inauguration ought to take place before the first of June. Still what is is, and I wouldn't hurt the figure. But I would certainly do all in your power to have the inauguration not after the first week in June for the figure's sake as well as your own.

I have been to the site for the Farragut at least fifty times, sometimes I think it is a bully site and sometimes I think a better one might be found. I have gone there with lots of people, and their opinions differ as much as mine do. There has been no need of hurrying about it, as we are sure of the site, and they won't begin laying the foundations before April. I have been on the point of writing that formal application to the Park Commissioners twice, but both times have been stopped, the last time by your letter saying there should be twenty-five feet from the sidewalk to the figure. This upset me, for in that site it can't be did. I went up with tape lines and found that it brought the figure just in the worst place and smack into the path. Your wife's letter, however, makes it all right.

I am very glad, nevertheless, that I was stirred up in my mind, for I have come myself to the almost decided conclusion that the 26th St. corner of Madison Park and 5th Ave. is a better place. It is more removed from the other statues and is altogether a more select, quiet and distinguished place, if it is not quite so public. It is in a sweller part of the Park, just where the aristocratic part of the Avenue begins and right opposite both Delmonico's and the Hotel Brunswick and the stream of people walking down Fifth Ave. would see it at once. It also would have a more northerly light and you wouldn't have any white reflections to dread.

Here is the whole plan of the Park. [sketch]

Here is a larger view of the end. [sketch] Now, if it were put here, I do not exactly know whether it would be best to place him cornerwise, as line A-B or parallel with the Avenue, as B-C. I myself prefer A-B. What do you think? Everybody I have asked favors the last site

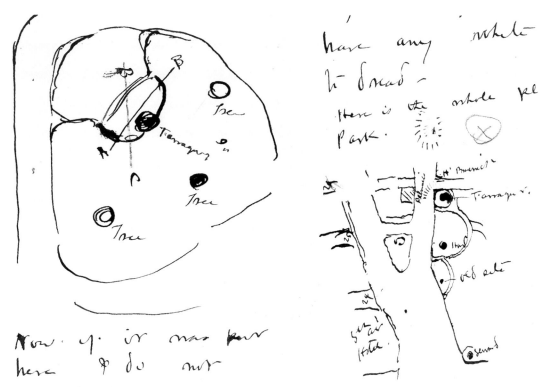

To Saint-Gaudens, February 24, 1880, showing the Farragut site at the northwest corner of Madison Square, 26th Street and Fifth Avenue

most. I will consult Olmsted and Cisco and Field, and, if they like it best, I will apply for it, if it is necessary, before hearing from you. If you strongly object, you must telegraph. I won't make the application before sixteen days. Write at once, however.

I will not telegraph you about the sea, but will write you—that is, unless you give reasons for my telegraphing you other than the need of getting the models here for the workmen to start cutting them.

What has become of the model for the cross? I hope you have decided about the Morgan's things. Prices are going up like lightning, and he will, I am afraid, be in a frightful rage.

You must think me a hell of a feller to be digging pins in you all the time this way.

Now I am going to bust you in the snout. What do you mean by writing Bunce that your sister would leave about a week after you wrote your letter and that she would arrive after about "a week or ten days" after he received 'this'. I immediately thought she had put off sailing a week. HOY? However, I went down to the Scythia, which arrived the day after your letter, and saw Miss Homer, and it took all my courage to do so, for I was sick as a dog, had a frightful cold and a nose on me as swollen as Bardolph's and as red as her own cheeks. She was the perfect picture of loveliness and health. I only saw her for a short time, as she was very well taken care of, and one is apt to be in the way in such cases. But I certainly mean some way or other to manage to get to Boston soon, not only for the pleasure of seeing her, but to ask the five hundred and fifty questions I wish to. All this ought to be written to your wife, indeed is. Give her my best regards; Louis also.

Ever lovingly thine.

[Signed with caricature]

MAY 8, 1880

DEAR OLD BOY:

I was darned glad to get your last of April 21st. Why in hell didn't you write me before! After the account I received of your sufferings I have been solemnly sitting on a picket fence imagining all sorts of things, and the day before I received your letter I wrote to Miss Eugenia to know how you was.

I am devilish glad you are coming home so soon. Let me see. You are going to sail on the 26th. I have then but one month more to write you. "Thank God!" I hear you saying.

I suppose you will have to give up your visit to Lille and the Low Countries. But do not miss a day at the South Kensington and a day at the British Museum. Be sure not to. It will fire you all up. Go to the Royal Academy, too, and see the early fellows there.

I will tell you now, as shortly as I can, what has happened about the Randall pedestal. I am getting sick and tired of writing you long accounts in which I seem to have had a devil of a trouble and a hell of a time, which is all damn nonsense.

Sometime in January I received a letter from Thomas Greenleaf, controller of Sailor's Snug Harbor, asking me to call on him in reference to the pedestal, which I did. I then made a sketch of a pedestal with a big seat behind it, showed it to Dix, who liked it: went down to Staten Island to see the site which I objected to at once; hobnobbed with the superintendent and got some points as to price, etc., from him.

Then I prepared for the Committee a drawing from our first sketch that I am sure would have come out well. The seat was about forty feet across. In

front of the pedestal was a long stone on which I thought you could put a relief of a yawl boat in a storm or something of the kind, and around the back of the seat there ran a bronze inscription. All this cost about seventy-five thousand dollars.

Also, to make sure, I prepared an alternative design, costing about forty-five thousand dollars.

I sent these two with a strong letter, insisting on your desire to have a horizontal line to oppose your perpendicular one, and strongly advocating blue-stone. So far everything had gone all right. Nothing had been said about your having to furnish the design, and I kept discreetly silent. But I knew Babcock was on the Committee and so did not go off on any exultation war-whoops to you. I knew him only too well. Six weeks passed. I received a let-ter from Dix asking me to meet him, Dr. Paxton and Mr. Babcock in reference to the pedestal. Dr. Paxton couldn't come, and I found, to my dismay, that Babcock led Dix around by the nose. I don't know whether you know Babcock. He is President of the Board of Commerce, one of the sharpest and mean-est business men in New York, a perfect blockhead about art, and the most pig-headed man I know of. In the first place they (he) did not want the seat, would not have it under any consideration. They (he) wanted a single pedestal like those in the Park. The Webster was the best. It's the damndest thing in the city. "Had I seen the Webster?" "No I hadn't." "Well, I'd better see it, as I could then form some idea of what they (he) wanted."

I thanked him and said I supposed that the reason they consulted me was to have something that you wanted, and in all cases that was what I proposed to

make. Babcock got red in the face, but Dix came to my support and said, "Precisely."

Babcock then said, "I suppose you know Mr. St. Gaudens' contract includes the design for the pedestal." I said, "Yes." He then read the contract and Dix chimed in with, "Oh, yes, I suppose of course Mr. White understands that. Indeed, Mr. St. Gaudens introduces him to me as his representative in his absence." He then read your letter, which unfortunately could be read both ways (though, of course, it made no difference). I said that that was a matter for them to settle with you. Then Babcock objected to bluestone and said the base must be of granite. They asked me to prepare a new design to be presented at next month's meeting of the board, and Babcock made the enlightened proposition that I need only make the sketch, as all 'these granite men' had draughtsmen in their employ who would make all the details, etc., etc., and save me a lot of trouble.

I thereupon in your name and mine distinctly refused to have anything to do with it, unless the work was to be carried out properly; and Dix again came to my assistance with "Precisely. I suppose the work will be cut under your direction."

"Certainly," I replied, "or not at all." Then I cleared out.

The second design I made as severe and simple as possible, one stone on top of another. I should have made it like your sketch in the photograph, but it had to be made in two stones on account of the enormous expense of one—as it is the approximate estimates came to four thousand six hundred dollars. Since sending the sketches, I have heard nothing from them. Perhaps they are disgusted with the plainness of the

design. If so, I should say as you have to furnish the design that that is a matter for you to settle. Perhaps Babcock is having 'one of his granite men who,' etc., carry out the design. If he has, I shall have the whole office of Evarts, Southmayd & Choate down on him. But this is not at all likely. They are probably like most committees—inactive. I shall stir Dix up and find out what has been settled on.

There; I've written you a long letter. Believe me, it is more trouble to write than I've been to in the whole affair. I enjoyed making the first designs and have them for my pains. Otherwise, save my contempt for Babcock, I have got along well with everybody. If the Committee so "graciously decide," I shall put the thing through, and if we can strike them for anything, well and good. But if you say anything more about "bill" to me, I'll retaliate on you in a way you least expect. I am writing this on the train between Newport and New York, which may account for its more than legible handwriting.

I cannot tell you how driven I am with business on account of McKim's absence from the office. For the last month I have been nearly frantic, being often at my office till midnight. Poor McKim is much better, but still unable to work. He will have to go abroad again. He will be devilish sorry to miss you. Damn strong-minded women, say I. I tell you, "You no catchee me marry."

Loads, heaps and piles of love to Louis and my sincere regards to your wife, whom I still owe a letter as well as other things, and to yourself the hug of a bear.

Lovingly,

[Signed with caricature]

NOTE

John A. Dix, former Governor of New York.

Samuel Denison Babcock (d. 1902), president and director, International Telephone Company; director, New York Central and Harlem Railroad and several New York banks; board member of most major cultural institutions in New York; member of the Farragut Monument Commission.

William Miller Paxton (1824–1904) minister and theologian who served as pastor of the First Presbyterian Church in New York and was on the faculty of Union Theological Seminary and Princeton Theological Seminary; trustee of Sailor's Snug Harbor.

MEXICAN TRIP

In 1882 Stanford White joined his brother, Dick, in New Mexico, where the latter was prospecting for gold. Throughout his life, White helped his brother financially, invested in his projects, and recommended him for jobs, but Dick seems to have been an ill-fated character. Judging from these letters, he was a rugged cowboy.

Besides writing to his parents, White also sent a long description of his adventures to Nelly Smith Butler, sister of his future wife, Bessie. McKim had introduced White to Bessie, whom he had met during the course of designing a house for Nelly and her husband, Prescott Hall Butler. Perhaps it was to impress the woman he was courting that White sent this long letter to her sister.

From New Mexico White travelled in Mexico and sketched Spanish colonial architecture.

House in Mexico

Stanford White (second from left) in Mexico

MARCH 2, 1882

MY DARLING MAMA,

For the love of Heaven send me my summer under-clothing. Letters, registered letter, box of instruments all received. Dick weighs 185 pounds and looks accordingly. I find him the same bully fellow he ever was—his face is the color of a Chinese lobster, and his vocabulary contains some choice selections of New Mexican grammar.

The cuisine here is rather limited—golly, for something good to eat. It is impossible to obtain here even a glass of milk or a fresh egg—everything is canned. The butter comes from Massachusetts and the meat from Missouri. We live in a shanty on the outskirts of the town. I wouldn't live at one of the hotels for a fortune. Bugs! Here at least we are free from them. I have stood the mountain trip pretty well and have had the start for a camping twice—colder than blazes. We have an old and experienced Indian scout with us, two Winchesters, a Sharp, two double-barrelled shotguns and four revolvers—to say nothing of Bowie knives and match boxes. There is almost as much danger of my being shot here as my being run over in New York, and of my being scalped

by the Indians as of my being smashed up in a railway collision. So your causes for anxiety are no way lessened, but then neither are they increased. If I come home in a pine box, I am sure it will be caused by Dick's style of living. I would give a hundred dollars to see your Joe here and see him cook a beefsteak. I am going to peg the next one and use it for the sole of my boot.

Send nothing down here—there's no place to put it. Dick has been swearing every day since I came here on account of the things I got at Park and Tilford's. We start for the Black Range soon, and may be gone three weeks—so do not get anxious.
Love to Papa,
    affly, Stan

NOTE

Park and Tilford was a fashionable sporting goods store in New York. McKim, Mead & White designed their uptown branch, at 72nd Street and Columbus Avenue, in 1892.

SOCORRO. MARCH 27, 1882
    DEAR PAPA,
I should have written you before, but I have had barely time to write mother, and I knew you would see the letters I wrote her. I have about now won my spurs from the charge of tenderfootism—as I have time and again now slept in the open air in storms, and have walked 40 miles in the day, been 14 hours in the saddle, and worked seven days solid ten hours' work with pick and drill. Dick still however insists that I am a "tenderfoot" because I insist on getting decent things to eat—if I can—he insists that leathery beefsteak must be stuck to whether better things can be obtained or not. This is an infernal country—it has no trees or water and generally looks like the entrance to Hell.

Life here is unquestionably dangerous, and he who comes here, or they who have friends or relatives here, must make up their minds to quietly accept the fact that he or they may be likely at any moment to change their abode suddenly. Still, so are we likely to do anywhere. There are only added dangers here, that is all—and as soon as the novelty wears off, you do not mind them any more than you do the dangers around you at home. I would not show Mama this.

The Indians are reported out again—but there is probably no truth in the story.

We go to the Black Range tomorrow, and I go from there for a short trip into Mexico. I shall write Mama a letter which will go with this, which you will see. I shall be out of reach of communication and writing now for probably 40 to 50 days. Glad to hear that you are so well.

    lovingly, Stan

Socorro 28th March

My Darling Mama —

Thunder is here

& have been sitting like patience
on a razor — thinking for the time
I should get back to town & could
put on my light underclothes
— & I get a letter from you saying
"do you really want your summer
underclothes" It is the coldest
thing ever happened to me — ~~~~~
I telegraphed to you & hope to find
them at El Paso — if I can
stop there — We got back
from the "Gallinas" all
right — & next out to the
"Sadornes" & got back all
night too — We start to day
Tuesday March 28th for the
Black range — they are 150
miles up & it will take us five
days & until Sat. April 1st to
get there — Dick stays there
all a month — I never will
not stay more than three or
four days & then shall go

To his mother, Socorro, March 28, 1882

STANFORD WHITE

MY DARLING MAMMA,

Thunder! Here I have been sitting like patience on a razor—thinking for the time I should get back to town and would put on my light underclothes, and I get a letter from you saying "do you really want your summer underclothes." It is the saddest thing ever happened to me. I telegraphed to you and hope to find them at El Paso, if I can stop there.

We got back from "Gallinas" all right, and went out to the "Sadsones" and got back all right too. We start today for the Black Range: they are 150 miles off, and it will take us five days, i.e. until Sat. April 1st to get there. Dick stays there about a month; I however will not stay more than three or four days, and then shall go to Mexico, passing through El Paso, Texas, about the 5th of April. We then stage it four days to Chihuahua, Mexico, where we stop a week. This will bring us to about the 15th April. We are then going over the Sierras to a little town called Batopilas, about 125 miles s.w. of Chihuahua. We shall take an Indian guide, and shall have to camp out altogether. It will take about a week to make the journey. We shall stay at the Batopilas for another week, and then return to Chihuahua, arriving there about the 1st to 5th May, and passing through El Paso on the way back about the 10th, arriving at Socorro again about the 12th. This is the arranged programme, but of course we may deviate from it—

but in any case I shall not be able to write and shall be out of communication for nearly 40 days. Write to El Paso unless you hear to the contrary from me up to the last week in April—after that to Socorro. I shall probably stay in Socorro until the latter part of May, and then go up to Oregon—to stay I do not know how long as yet.

I am sorry Kate is going to leave—what will you do without her? Be sure to give her a present from me and my best wishes, and tell her I can bake cakes as well as she can now. I had hoped to write you a long letter as to what we were doing, but I have just time to scratch this off. By the way, there are two photograph books—one of old pictures, and the other of old English houses and furniture, in my room: please send them to the office. I am glad to hear you are all so well. I am all right and have begun to gain in weight—Dick is always well.

I have had little or no time to hunt since I have been here, but have been after deer two or three times with good and bad luck. I am going bear-trailing in the Black Range. There is one advantage of this infernal country, and that is that the sky is blue six days out of seven. Charley is a first-rate companion, and is going to teach me Spanish; and we are both going to marry a couple of Mexican girls and forget to bring them away with us. Keep well, and be sure and not worry.

Lovingly, Stan

TO MRS. PRESCOTT HALL BUTLER
BLACK RANGE, PALOMAS VALLEY
APRIL 12, 1882

DEAR MADAME PRESCOTT:

I have been doing some pretty tough work in a pretty tough country, and so my letter would have been colored like the landscape which abounds here—*toujours* grey, tinged off into sulphurous and most unchristian purples and greens. Now you do not like that sort of thing, do you? Nor I. So I have waited until now, where, being amongst green grass and green trees and playing hookey as I am, my frame of mind is a little more seraphic than force of circumstances here have so far allowed it to be.

So here I am, under the shade of a huge juniper, scribbling to you. I am scout until midday, and then have engaged to hunt for dinner. I am to bring home anything I choose, but hares, certainly. Do you think I will get them? If I do not, I shall lay it all to you. Were it civilized, it would be hard to imagine a more lovely spot than this—and even as it is, it is lovely enough. As a general rule, however, New Mexico is an awful hole. There is neither water nor wood here; the fodder is beyond belief; and as for "buggies"—do not mention them. They are here of all kinds and sizes, and numberless, and the greatest "hardship" one can be put to is to have to go to a hotel—Brrr!!!

The quality of the air is almost perfect; "it never rains and the sky is always blue"—but a "gentle" sirocco blows often at the rate of thirty miles an hour. The dust is unbearable, and it rather upsets your ideas of the eternal fitness of things to have the thermometer 90 degrees in the shade at noon, and find ice water *au natural* in your canteens next morning. This is almost an invariable occurrence, and

sometimes makes sleeping with nothing but Heaven for a canopy somewhat unpleasant. One morning we found our blankets frozen to the ground, and my nose, my nose—it seemed like solid ice. But the devil is not so black as he is painted, and now and then you come across cases such as this; and I do now believe, although I had doubts of it before, that the Lord had something to do with the creation of this country.

General Sherman hit the nail on the head when he was asked, after returning from his tour of inspection, "what he thought of the country." "Think!," he said, "I think the best thing we can do is to give them (Mexico) a thundering good thrashing and make them take it back again."

For the first time since we have been here, we have struck a running stream. There are five of them here, and they gurgle and splash away, all joining together about a mile below and forming the Polomas River—which rushes through the Canyon, and then disappears into the sands forever.

The Black Hills are what they call here the "Continental Divide." They are in fact the end spurs of the Rocky Mountains, and they make a good stand in this country of interminable sands for the land they belong to. This is quite historical ground: here Vittoria, after having given up his lands to the Government and gone to Mexico, returned, saying he would live or die on his old stamping-ground—and about twenty months ago, in the valley below was fought the battle which ended in the extermination of his whole tribe. They call the place by the classic name of "Skull and Bones Gulch." Do you want any for Parlor Ornaments! They can be had for the picking up.

STANFORD WHITE

The ghosts of the slain still hover around—for we lead a garrison's life at the cabin. There have been all manner of reports flying about, but without foundation. There have been no signs of Indians as yet, and this excessive precaution is rather exasperating. Still, I suppose the boys are right: three little piles of stone at the back of the cabin are rather sharp reminders. They had a pretty rough time of it here last year, and they are naturally suspicious of such infernal devils, who can travel so like a whirlwind. They have been twice surprised here, the Apaches making the journey from their reservation, 97 miles off, in one night. We struck our tents inside of a sort of stone fort the first night, but we are all together now, in a log cabin and stockade built last year. This is rather different from the style of domicile we have been enjoying, where we have had but the prairie for a house, and have slept like the Kings of France at St. Denis, all in a row. [sketch]

It is much pleasanter than you would imagine, but a little unsafe, for in spite of the fact that we lie down with eight rifles and shot guns, six revolvers, and four Bowie knives—to say nothing of a dozen pounds or so of giant powder and our tooth-picks—still, as we sleep the sleep of the just, if anybody chose to take a ground shot at us, it would be unpleasant, to say the least. To be sure, there is our "dawg" Rover, and I beg his pardon for forgetting him; I would draw his picture, but I can't. He is a Scotch Collie, and the best dog I have ever seen—but his chief accomplishment, as far as I have ever seen, is a really wonderful ability to tackle the business end of a mule. He looks upon them and wolves as his natural enemies, and makes furious charges on them at night; much to my discomfort, as I have gone through, in consequence, all the terrors of

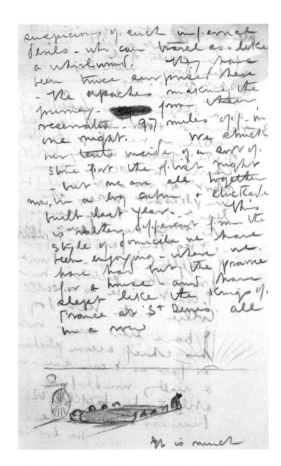

Sketch of the campers sleeping "like the Kings of France at St. Denis"

an Indian surprise—at least half a dozen times. They all laugh at me for this, and there is a tradition in camp that when the Indians really do come, Rover sets all the guns at full cock, gently gnaws you ear, gives one long low howl, and then incontinently "skins out"—which latter instance of sagacity your humble servant intends to follow to the letter.

It was a tedious journey here from Socorro and took us six days. But in spite of the monotony, there is something wonderful and almost mysterious about the great plains. The one the southern end of which we crossed—the St. Augustine Plain—is a "mesa" nearly seven thousand feet in the air, and is forty miles wide and more than a hundred long. It is all sand and thin grass, and looks like some vast inland sea, with ranges of mountains dropping behind the horizon like ships half hull-down. [sketch]

It is funny to have boyish dreams come to pass. I often used to wonder at and think what queer feelings must sometimes have crossed the Spanish adventurers in their long tramp. With the thermometer at 100°, and water thirty miles off, the romance was rather taken out of it. Yet in spite of this, you could not help feeling something like a Grandee in search of the Seven Cities of Gold, after a day or two of this sort of thing [sketch] and whenever we reached a rise, I could not resist the temptation of spurring my horse to see what was on the other side. The last day out, we made over the old Indian trail, and the wagon containing our grub broke down, and my brother had to ride sixty miles, there and back, to a blacksmith's to get new bolts. We live on the fat of the land here: deer, wild turkey, wild pigeon, and "bear steak" if you want it. I shot at one Tuesday, but I was afraid to shoot until I had waded the river, and as he was more frightened than I was, he had got beyond my marksmanship—fortunately for me, perhaps.

The Mexicans are the meanest people, certainly, I have ever met, and the country is full of scamps and rascals. Fortunately I have had little to do with them, but have met, and been with, a body of men who, although somewhat roughened by their life are still the best of fellows and companions. They are daring and courageous to a fault, and absolutely without nonsense of any kind, and intolerant of it in others. Most of them are engineers or miners—and if they are determined and resolute, they are equally kind-hearted and hospitable. They will share their bread with a perfect stranger, and risk life and property to aid a comrade. There is a certain unobtrusive heroism about it all which makes you think of Elevated Railroad jobbing and afternoon receptions, with a little contempt, now and then. Still, that is poor philosophy: one can be as courageous or cowardly there as here. The only difference is that you are apt to be found out here at once.

I think I had better shut up on moralizing. I must stop anyway, and will try to finish this tonight in the cabin.

What do you think of me as a cook? The boys think I am a pretty poor one, which I don't mind: but it makes me mad to be such a poor shot and rider, when they are all such splendid ones. Still, I am getting along pretty well, and have learnt many things useful for a bachelor to know. I have even washed my own clothes; they did not come very white—but we are not proud here. Adieu.

This is six days later, and I am a nice fellow, am I not! I have been through a lot of "hair-breadth escapes!!" since writing the above. I am now in Mexico. I am going to Chihuahua and then to Batopilas, a town on the Pacific slope of the Sierras. It will be a six-hundred-mile journey there and back on mules. Coming from the Black Range we travelled sixty hours with but five hours sleep, and I felt like a daisy in June afterward.

I do not expect to be back till the Fall, unless Charles is unwell or McK M & W wish me back. I shall come home, however, if I do not go to Oregon. I hope to have a long loaf now. We have heard all manner of stories about Chihuahua! "Fruit and flowers, birds and butterflies flying about, bees stinging, etc. and black eyed senoritas." I shall leave the last to my companion, who is a peripatetic son of a Quaker who makes shot and owns the big yellow tower in Duane St. There are pigs in the house I am writing in. Remember me kindly to everyone, and believe me ever and always your friend and servant,

[Signed with monogram]

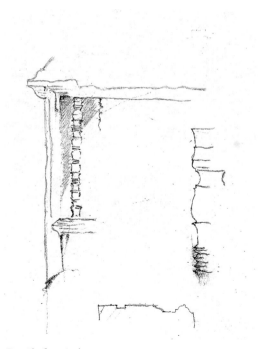

Detail of a window

APRIL 14, 1882

MY DARLING MAM,

Arrived all right in Chihuahua, and am now a hundred miles on the road to Batopilas. We found that it would be a six-hundred mile journey on mule-back, there and back, and so took advantage of some friends' offer of an ambulance to go this far. We are now in a Heaven-forsaken hole named "Carnchic," and are waiting for mules; we have cursed ourselves hoarse in bad Spanish, but cannot get our mules before tomorrow morning. Hang it, I have done nothing but sleep on stone floors in hovels of stone since I left Chihuahua— golly, I will be glad to get back to the open air and our own cooking—jerked beef, ow' ow' ow'. It is only one hundred and fifty miles from Chihuahua to Batopilas, so you see what a mountainous journey it must be to spin out to double the length. We make two sheer descents of six thousand feet this way: [sketch]

I am surprised to find that there is a chance of getting a mail into the States. This awaits a courier, and I do not know when you will get it. Dick was well and happy when I left him; I will join him again about the 12th or 15th of May.

It takes an ordinary letter 5 days to get to El Paso, but a registered letter takes 15 days. The underclothes I suppose are there by this time, but of course I did not get them.

Love to Papa,

Affly, Stan

BATOPILAS. APRIL 26, 1882

MY DEAR PAPA,

It is too hot to write or do anything. It is either that, or, profiting by the example of those around me, I have inhaled the inherent laziness of the country. You never saw such people—the Italians are nothing to them. They live from day to day, perfectly satisfied with enough to eat, and a crust for the moment. Any surplus is immediately gambled away—and I heard a most ingenious argument the other day in favor of gambling as a national blessing—as otherwise, nobody could do any work. And yet they can work if they will—their power of endurance is much greater than ours. A Mexican courier will make the distance from here to Chihuahua, 300 miles, inside of five days, carrying fifty pounds and taking with him as food only a bag of "pinole," or Indian meal. The miners here also will outwork the Yankees.

We made part of our journey here in a stage; the balance, 180 miles, we did on muleback in four days and two hours, which was very fair time. I was pretty tired and stiff, and my mule more so. Our Mosos, or runners, however were quite fresh. The Indians whom we met and who inhabit the Sierras are perfectly harmless and the most peaceful set of people in the world. They generally stampeded the moment they clapt eyes on us. Their costume is practically nakedness, and some of them had perfectly splendid figures. The trip was a most beautiful one, and the country quite like that at home. It is a high table land broken up into mountains, valleys and plains, full of water and wood, up-hill, down-dale, over seemingly impassable precipices and by the side of beautiful streams. One time we wound five hours through an "arroya" by the side of a small river, and again the trail led through a continuous pine forest, 15 miles long, on a "mesa" eight thousand feet in the air and flat as a board. This lasted until the evening of the day before the last of our journey. We then crossed the divide, reaching an elevation of about nine thousand feet. Next day the scene changed utterly—to one of tremendous and desolate grandeur; and we spent the whole day in one steady descent to Batopilas—and practically the tropics.

We are the guests here of Gov. Sheppard at the Hacienda, and are treated with every consideration and kindness. It was rather unexpected, and I was utterly unprepared for petticoats and champagne in this latitude, and have nothing but old clothes to wear, and so feel somewhat uncomfortable.

There is one thing I am sadly disappointed in—the fruit is not ripe here yet, and will not be before I leave, which will be in a week or so. There is a fine river to bathe in, though—plenty of mules to ride, and the sport in the Sierras is as good as one could wish. I should have got four deer yesterday morning; but either because my rifle was not a long-range one, or because I am not a good enough shot, I only got two. I find 200 yards is quite enough for me to manage.

I shall get back to Socorro about the 20th of May. I am not going to Oregon, and so shall be home sooner than I expected. I enclose a letter to Anais Casey—please see that it is sent to her wherever she is.

Love to Mama,

affly, Stan

Batopilas
Apr 26th /82

My Dear Papa.
It is too hot to write —
or do anything. It is either that or —
profitting by the example of these around —
me I have inhaled the inherent laziness
of the country. You never saw such
people — the Italians are nothing to
them. They live from day to day.
— perfectly satisfied with enough to eat
+ a cigar for the moment. Any surplus
immediately is gambled away — and
I heard a most ingenious argument
the other day in favor of gambling
as a natural blessing — as otherwise
nobody would do any work. And
yet they can work if they will —
Their power of endurance is much
greater than ours. A Mexican
courier will make the distance from
here to Chihuahua . 300 miles
inside of five days — carrying fifty
pounds — + taking with him as
food — only a bag of "pinole" or Indian

COURTSHIP & MARRIAGE

The letters from Stanford White to Bessie Smith begin during their courtship. In 1883, White writes once again from the West, where he travelled to see Dick, accompanied by Saint-Gaudens, and then joined one of his wealthiest patrons, the financier Henry Villard, in Portland, Oregon.

Bessie Smith and Stanford White were married at the Church of the Heavenly Rest in New York on February 7, 1884. Bessie was one of five daughters of Judge J. Lawrence Smith of Smithtown, Long Island. Her family had settled in the Smithtown area about 1650 and was proud of it; they were and still are extremely attached to their land. Bessie's mother, Sarah Nicoll Smith, was a Clinch from New York. Her aunt Cornelia had married A. T. Stewart, the department store magnate. Since the Stewarts were childless, Cornelia's five nieces became their heirs. Ultimately this legacy enabled Stanford and Bessie to purchase the land known as Carman Hill and expand the farmhouse into the manor they called Box Hill.

After the wedding White writes again to his mother during their first short honeymoon in the South and later to his parents and his sister-in-law Nelly from their grand tour of Europe.

Bessie did not retain many of the letters Stanford wrote during the twenty-two years of their marriage. The few that survive are concerned with the running of Box Hill, Larry's well-being, and White's social activity in New York. The final letters to Bessie allude to the economies he was forced to make at the end of his life and to the disastrous fire of 1905 that destroyed many of the works of art he planned to sell at auction.

The last letters in this collection, one written only a month before White was shot, are to Saint-Gaudens. He was ill with cancer and had retired to New Hampshire where he died in 1907.

Church at Presles, France

NEW YORK. SEPTEMBER 20, 1880

DEAR MISS BESSIE

Do you remember the discussion we had about the possibility of finding Oudin's little song?

I tried in half a dozen music stores without success, and was rather amused to come across it in an old ballad book of my father's, the songs of which I knew much better when I was two years old than I do now.

I have had it copied in the highest style of decorative art and—ahem!—beg you will accept it with all etc., etc.

I shall ask as a reward that you sing it to me the first time opportunity offers.

Remember me most kindly to your mother and Miss Ella, and believe me,

Very sincerely yrs, Stanford White

DEAR MR. WHITE,

How can I thank you for the basket of delicious fruit which I received last evening and above all for the touching little song which you had copied so beautifully for me? It will be my duty and pleasure to learn and practice the song all day, though I am sure the reward you ask will not be at all worthy of the trouble you took in getting it for me.

Hoping to see you soon,

Very sincerely yours, Bessie S. Smith

NEW YORK. FEBRUARY 1882

TO BESSIE SMITH

I had hoped that perhaps an opportunity might have come when I could have told you quietly what I said so abruptly last night—but if I could have gone silently without troubling you, it would have been but as I wished. Yet could I do that? No—for your sake more than my own. I have had to make a reasonable pretext for leaving, and I felt that if I delayed much longer telling Prescott and Nelly and my friends, their suspicions might be aroused at my going so suddenly. How much they suspect I do not know but I have told them nothing. To my partners, indeed, I was forced to give strong reasons for leaving them but beyond them no one, not even my mother, knows anything—save that I go on a vacation—except perhaps Ella—as I have been weak enough to drop one or two despairing words to her, in lack of all other sympathy—for which I beg you will forgive me.

After your last letter I furiously resolved that I would not again take advantage of what you told me was but weakness on your part—and now, dearest—

[Conclusion lost.]

To Bessie Smith, February 1882

COURTSHIP & MARRIAGE

MY DEAR PAPA,

I have just come from killing my first salmon—under somewhat exciting circumstances. Sport was good here up to the 4th, the day of our arrival; there were twenty-two salmon taken by eight rods on that day. Since then the average has been three a day, to many more rods—the reason being that the weather has been hot and clear, and the salmon also are beginning to play out. So I got my Indians this morning to put the boat on top of a freight train, and went ten miles up the river to try my luck there. When we got off, I discovered to my horror that the men had forgotten the gaff—and what is more, that one of them had lost his hat off the top of the car, with all the leaders and flies in it. So there was nothing to do but get in the canoe and shoot down the river home again—as trying to get a salmon without a gaff is like shooting a Buffalo with a pea-shooter.

I had an extra leader and fly in my pocket, and as we passed a most gorgeous pool, I made the men stop, and made a cast, just for fun. The fly lit on the water, and just as I whipped it out to throw again—a great thirty-pounder rose at it, three feet in the air. He took the second throw right in his mouth and away he rushed boiling through the water and making my reel sing F sharp for half a minute. Here was a pretty kettle of fish with a huge salmon on my line and no gaff to kill him—so I settled down to hard work and played the beast for three mortal hours—until I was nearly ready to drop. I had sent one of the Indians to see if he could not get something or other, and just as I was giving out, he came up with an old broken pitchfork—so he stoned the fish into a fury, and as I reeled him in, the Indian rushed into the water and jabbed him with the pitchfork. It was the greatest fun I ever had.

I am going into the wilderness tomorrow and expect lots of fish. All well—love to Mama,

Affly, Stan

NOTE

The Ristigouche Salmon Club, on the Gaspé Penninsula in Quebec Province, was considered by many to be pre-eminent among gentlemen's sporting clubs.

STANFORD WHITE

BETWEEN ST. LOUIS AND KANSAS CITY.

MY DARLING BESS,

It is so hot and dusty and miserable today that it hardly seems fair to be writing to one so lovely and fresh as thyself.

A most amusing thing happened just now. We were honored with having a Dining Car hitched on our train for a few hours, and were invited thereto by a youth resplendent, in spite of the dust, in a new white waistcoat and diamond pin. Having seated ourselves, we were approached by a very frisky looking darkey, who jauntily threw his napkin over his arm, bent his head down, and in this touching attitude awaited our orders. We gave them, and amongst other things ordered a bottle of wine. He soon reappeared, shifted his napkins to his shoulder, and deftly inserted a nosegay in St. Gaudens's buttonhole. He then did the same thing to me. "Is this thrown in?" I asked. "Oh yes sah, yes sah! Enterprise of the Co. sah! We presents every gent that orders wine with a Bokay, sah!" This is the sole event that has enlivened a stupid day. St. Gaudens swears that we have been passing the same cornpatch and fence for the last seven hours. Did I say a stupid day? I wronged thee, Bess: I have but to turn my thoughts inward, and I can find there enough happiness to illumine a prison. For do you not love me, my darling?

KANSAS.

I wonder, dear Bess, what you are doing now: up to some mischief, I'll be bound. I have been—I have been telling St. Gaudens the reason of my idiotic smiles and that my troubles are all over; to which he answered—after a preliminary dance around the car— that, *au contraire*, they had just begun! He is a brute, is he not! But I consoled myself with the thought that thou, my sweetheart, were somewhat different from his cross-grained clothes-rack of a frau. That was ungenerous, wasn't it as he had only seen you once, I showed him your "pictur," and he patted me on the back and told me that thou wast very very lovely (I would have chucked him out of the window if he had not) and then he said that he was glad that I would be myself again: that I had been cross and moody and ill-mannered and unbearable for the last three years, and that if I did not reform now, he would thump me well. So, Mademoiselle, you see what a task you have before you—I should not wonder, though, that you had accomplished the most of it already.

We have been running through one vast prairie all day long, the boundary of which has ever been the horizon: a constant accompaniment of telegraph poles and an occasional cow alone varying the monotony.

There is a high old thunderstorm going on at the present moment, in the midst of which I am going to turn over and dream of thee. Good night, my darling,

MY DARLING BESS,

I have just shaken the dust of New Mexico off my feet. We left there yesterday at the unchristian hour of three in the morning, and are now bowling over the Arizona Prairies towards Los Angeles. I do not think your opinion of "that horrid country" would have improved much had you been with us. Mine certainly would have, but I think thy tranquil heart would have been rather disturbed: we have had quite enough excitement to last us to the end of the trip.

I said good-bye to thee last Sunday. Monday morning at three o'clock we arrived at Engle. This may seem to you a very innocent statement, but I assure you it is not. It was here last year that I came very near getting a bullet hole through me because I was too tardy in accepting an invitation to drink. Engle is situated in the very midst of the "houmardo del muerto" (journey of death), a vast and howling desert over 300 miles long and 100 wide; and why either town or man should exist there, Heaven only knows. My brother fortunately was at the station to meet us. We were conducted to a sort of mud hut where the unwary traveller is expected to "put up," and were assigned to our rooms—I got along very well—but St. Gaudens, who is rather fresh at such business, was rather aghast to find two men in full possession of his apartment. He told me that one was a fierce looking footpad who muttered in his sleep; both of them slept armed to the teeth, and St.

Gaudens lay down on the outside of his bed in "full dress," momentarily expecting to be murdered. About four o'clock an awful row began: wild screams of fire were heard and we all rushed out in various states of dress and undress to find that the store, filled with miners' supplies, was in a sheet of flame. The building was rather a large one, and it constituted singly and solely the town of Engle: and in the blackness of the night and the desolation of the vast prairie it was a pretty appalling sight. To make matters worse, no one dared to go near the building, as it contained all manner of explosives and a fifty-pound box of giant powder—which, had it gone off, would have blown us all to atoms. But there was an even chance that it would only burn: so although we all secretly had the fiercest desire to run like blazes, pride and curiosity kept us by.

The cartridges soon began to go off, and for an half an hour it was like a sharp battle, the pistol and rifle cartridges exploding like the rattle of infantry, and now and then a giant cartridge going off like canon. The wind slightly veered and the corral began to smoke; and in an instant, in spite of the danger, twenty men had burst in the doors, torn down the fence and run the stage and cattle out—my brother, as usual, being first to lead. If it had been last year I would not have been far behind him; but I thought of thee, and that I would not lose going back to thee for all the corrals in Mexico—so I hid behind an adobe wall. They had hardly got the cattle out when

a keg of black powder went off with a frightful explosion—and the wildest stampede occurred. One man ran more than two thousand yards out into the prairie before he stopped.

During all this time there were a dozen boys at least howling, donkeys braying, cattle and horses chiming in; and to cap the climax, two bears that had been captured and chained roared with all their might. Such a bedlam of sound I never heard. But—this giant did not explode—or I should not have been writing you this.

Next morning we started off for the mountains, going thirty miles over the prairie to Chucillo Negro, and thence on horseback to the Palomas, thirty miles again. The sun was something terrible—it fairly baked me to a cinder. After the first ten miles St. Gaudens, I think, wished he had not come—and before another ten miles had been ridden, he was completely exhausted—but we could not stop, as it was becoming dark. When we got to the canyon, it was so black we could hardly see the trail. St. Gaudens fainted before we got to my brother Dick's cabin, but fortunately it was only for a moment, and we managed to get him there and bolstered him up on Liebig's Extract and whiskey. The next day he was too used up to do anything, so we stretched our program and stayed a day longer.

That evening (Tuesday) we camped out. It was the first time St. Gaudens had ever slept in the open air,

and as we told a few "Ber" and panther stories over the camp-fire, one of the boys casually remarked that "snakes sometimes crawled over you." He passed his night in trepidation and stark staring wakefulness. I woke for a moment about two at night, and he said: "Is that you, Stan?" "For heaven's sake, how much longer are you fellows going to lie here!"

The next morning we went out deer hunting. There was only one shot, and I did not shoot him, or thou should have the tail. But the hunt was very funny—be sure to remind me to tell you about it. The next day (yesterday) was the greatest lark of all. We came all the way from Chloride to Engle (60 miles) by stage. The driver was the most successfully drunk man I have ever seen. He ran his horses down the mountain and nearly threw us in the canyon half a dozen times, and the shindy ended by his telling St. Gaudens Hewasbebemoshsleepisheverwas—taketh reins—and he deposited the reins in St. Gaudens' hands and fell into the boot, leaving St. G. (we were all inside) who had never driven in his life, master of the situation with four lively steeds on his hands and half the prairie to cover. But he did it nobly and brought us in half an hour ahead of time: and so ended our adventures.

It is a funny country—you cannot imagine the desolation of the landscape in and about the prairie, nor the absolute loveliness.

Wedding portrait of Bessie Smith White by Saint-Gaudens. The Metropolitan Museum of Art, New York. Gift of the Erving Wolf Foundation, 1976 (1976.388).

STANFORD WHITE

SEPTEMBER 11, 1883

MY DARLING BESS.

The four days are up, and I have not written thee a word, nor did I go to church yesterday at all. I couldn't —I was wedged in between a villainous looking Californian and a still more villainous Oregonian, and the contamination would have been too great. Still, four thousand miles is not much for the imagination to skip over, and about eleven o'clock my thoughts began to follow a certain raven-haired puss in her devotions, when I suddenly remembered that I had promised to conduct myself strictly within the lines of common sense, and that though it was eleven here it was one o'clock on Long Island, and that the aforesaid puss was probably eating her dinner; so I became material and wished that I was going to get as good a dinner as she was eating. Alas! That I had!

I wrote you last Tuesday night—very late. Very early Wednesday morning we arrayed ourselves in fighting trim, seized our deadly weapons and departed on the path of gore and glory. We ran up through the valley of the Sacramento to the end of the northern line of the C.P.R.R., passed the night at Redding, and the next morning pranced off on two fiery Pegasuses, which outshone Rosinante in beauty and Ercole in speed. Why were not you, dear Bess, who love the country so, with us? You cannot imagine such lovely scenery. The trail led out of the great valley yellow with grain, over a series of low mountains and through small valleys watered with the most lovely rushing streams, and filled with great pine forests, the quiet of which was disturbed only by the notes of the wood pigeon and thrush; and then past Mt. Shasta, who soars nearly 15,000 feet into Heaven

in solitary grandeur, and—well, that's enough! We did not get any farther than that—I will return to our starting place.

I told thee that our steeds were fiery, did I not. The whole distance between the lines is about 210 miles, which I had intended to make in four days. St. Gaudens, remembering his New Mexico experience said "not much!" The liveryman said not only "not much" but that there was not a horse in Siskiyou County who could make it—but it had to be made, someway, as I had to meet Mr. Villard in Portland on Monday the 11th. So we sharpened our spurs, got on our steeds and trusted to Providence. The first day we rode 32 miles, and St. G. said he would not ride another for all the Kings of Egypt. The second day we got over 27 miles before noon, which was doing splendidly; but while we were resting after lunch it was our fell luck to have a couple of Indians come along, one of whom had two hats on, a straw over a plug, with a feather in it. He had, besides this, one leg of a pair of trousers on, and the other leg bare, and a red sash around his waist, and in this picturesque attire was a study to the believer in the noble savage. He had with him a great string of over fifty trout, which he assured us he had just caught in the stream; and he offered to sell us either the fish or his hook and lines—at about five times their market value. Fired by noble ambition, we invested in the lines, spent the whole afternoon fishing, and caught—three fish! Much crestfallen, we determined to get up very early next morning and put in the biggest day's horsebackriding yet done by man. We did get up early—about four o'clock—and started off at a rattling pace. After I had gone about four miles, I discovered I had left my cartridge belt, bowie knife and pistol behind me. So I gallopped hard back again for them; and when I had caught up with St. G. my horse was not fresher for the adventure. We had not gone ten miles further when St. Gaudens found that he had dropped his auxiliary rifle-barrel out of its case on the road. So he gallopped back. He could not find it. It was now near midday, and our horses were sweating; so we turned in for lunch at the base of Mount Shasta, which had gradually been coming into sight. We had made but 17 miles that morning, and took a long siesta looking at the mountain, so things were beginning to look pretty scary—when what was our horror to find, on going to the barn, that both our horses had all gone to pieces—mine lamed up in both legs, and St. Gaudens's with a sore back. So we gave up the ghost and waited for the stage. Do you know what that means? All night and all day and all next night cramped up against your neighbor—no chance to sleep, rattling over a stony mountain road, and twenty minutes for meals. If you ever hear of anybody bemoaning the old stage-coach times, let them try the Oregon and California stages, and they will forever after hold their peace.

When the stage came up it was full—but that made no difference. Three were squeezed in a seat intended for two. My neighbors were a very pretty girl and a very ugly old woman. The pretty girl, alas, got out at the next station but her place was supplied by the aforesaid villainous Californian, and the old lady remained. She was asthmatic, and groaned and wheezed and complained the live long night. She had a bird and a band-box, two shawls and a satchel, which she kept alternately depositing in everybody's lap—and sometimes she would put herself there—or rather, the jolting of the stage would. She insisted on

getting out at every station, upsetting the whole stage by doing so, and it took three or four of us hauling on her in front and pushing her from behind to get her back again. Now and then there would come a terrible jounce, and we would all be shot out of our seats and meet together in the top of the stage. It was great fun. We got rid of petticoats by dawn, and were more comfortable thereafter.

Sunday (yesterday) afternoon the stage broke down, and we thought we were done for—but they patched it up and made up time by tearing over bumpy roads and down mountains where the slightest tip would have sent us into canyons thousands of feet deep—in a way that would have curdled your blood. But here I am on the train, and we shall be in Portland this afternoon.

NOTE

Henry Villard controlled a network of rail and shipping lines in the Northwest, which he consolidated into the Northern Pacific Railroad in 1881. He then embarked on an ambitious building program that focused on freight and passenger terminals and a grand hotel in Portland to attract tourists to the West. Villard, however, was forced to resign from the Northern Pacific Railroad in 1884 and none of McKim, Mead & White's designs were ever executed. Villard was also forced to sell the elegant complex of houses the firm had designed for him on Madison Avenue and 51st Street in New York.

STANFORD WHITE

four months it had been entirely covered with smoke - & the very day that old H.V. came with his party the smoke cleared off & the mountain shone out in all its glory - the mist cut off the bottom entirely from the earth - & the

Mount Rainier

mountain actually looked as if it belonged to another world - I never saw anything like it - but what is the use of trying me to explain such things -

PORTLAND, OREGON

MY DARLING BESS,

I write you this while I am gnawing my nails with impatience at not getting thy letter. I have been awfully busy since I arrived here last Monday. Tuesday I saw his royal highness Mr. Villard. I do not know whether the papers have been full of him and his party in New York—but here you think of nothing else. The whole air is full of it: if he was a King there could not be more of a row.

I came here on business and have kept clear of the whole affair as much as possible— but I had to go up to Tacoma with him and his collection of English and Yarmen Dukes, Countesses, and high cockalorums generally. I cannot say I was much impressed, and I think myself just as good as any————old Lord in his party—don't you? The next time you catch me walking behind a brass band you will hear of it.

Portland is not an interesting place, and it is lucky that I am busy. St. G. is nearly dying of ennui. The splendid scenery all around here is completely enveloped in smoke. We were awfully lucky though up in Tacoma. Tacoma, by the way, is a God-forsaken place at the end of Puget Sound. It consists chiefly of board shanties and tree stumps—and this is what they call the coming metropolis of the Far West! Bah! Spread Eagle all around, and nothing but Spread Eagle. But at Tacoma, Puget Sound commences and it is a lovely sheet of water: and way above the town Mt. Ranier soars into the skies. It knocks Shasta higher than a kite: you get the full height, 14,440 feet, from the water's edge, and it is covered with eternal snow. For four months it had been entirely covered with smoke; and the very day that old H.V. came with his party, the smoke cleared off and the mountain shone out in all its glory. The mist cut off the bottom entirely from the earth, and the mountain actually looked as if it belonged to another world. [sketch] I never saw anything like it—but what is the use of trying to explain such things.

The next time I come out here, thou art to come with me: and we will go to the Yellowstone and Yosemite and have a gay time generally; and I will have a much gayer time than I otherwise could, for thou, my little puss, will be with me. I am not going this time: I am sick of the West and sick for a sight of thee. Boohoo! I wantter go home—and home I am coming as soon as I can. I may take a couple of days to see if I can not get thee a pair of elk horns; but I am not sure what I am going to do, save that I shall be at St. Paul about the 27th and home the 1st of October.

STANFORD WHITE

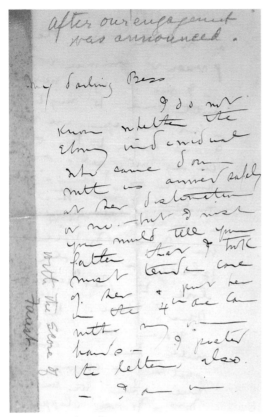

To Bessie Smith, Fall 1883

MY DARLING BESS,

I do not know whether the ebony individual who came down with us arrived safely at her destination or no—but I wish you would tell your father that I took most tender care of her and put her in the 4th Ave. car with my own hands. I posted the letters also.

I am in a whirl at the present moment. I wish you were with me tonight but as you are not, I am going to try to enjoy myself as much as I can—see and look for two—imagine you in Mrs. Bobbie's place, and make love to her "accordion" hair. Never mind—we will hear it soon together, and enjoy it more than ten hundred Mrs. Bobbies clapped together. Meanwhile, cherie, here is the score [of Faust] and if I ever sing to thee any less fervently than Faust did to his Marguerite, twill be—ah, no!—not thy fault—but it will not be mine.

I will meet you at the ferry, and we will go to the Hoss Show in the morning or afternoon, just as you choose. If you have no choice, let us say morning. As for my mother, she is ready to see you at any and all times—middle of the night if you choose. If you can, let us go on a spree in the evening—Ella and you and I and C.C. and Prescott and my mother if you think best: but she is not over well. My Daddy is better. Gimme a kiss and be a good girl. Goodbye until Wednesday morning.

ever thy loving,

[Signed with a caricature]

FEBRUARY 4, 1884

MY DARLING MAMA,

I hardly had any time to speak to you before I went
off—but we will have plenty of time before I sail. I
do not wish you to think that you are in the least bit
less to me now than before I was married. If you have
any troubles, you must always tell them to me, and
you may be sure I will do everything in my power to
help you, and it will be your own fault if you do not
tell me. You have indeed gained a very lovely daughter, and you must always think of me, dear mama,
now and ever, as your loving son

Stanford White

ON TRAIN BETWEEN CHARLESTON & SAVANNAH
FEBRUARY 11TH, 1884

MY DARLING MAMA,

Here we are—happy as two Long Island clams at
high water—tearing through Georgia pine forests:
the thermometer 75 in the shade, the air balmy, green
trees all around us and strawberries in blossom. The
fruit of the country seems chiefly to consist of small
niggers, always on a fence. We are in fact in Dixie
Land—and a very pleasant land it has proved to be
so far. In a few moments we will be in Savannah, and
by tomorrow in Jacksonville, which will be our headquarters for the short time we shall be in Florida; so
direct all communications there until the 19th.

We have had nothing to mar our pleasure since we
started. Bess is in the best of health and spirits,
although now and then somewhat tired, as any girl I
should think would be, with so much constant jour-
neying; but that will be all over tomorrow.

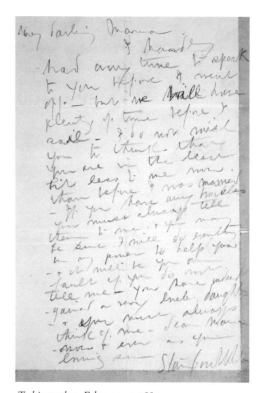

To his mother, February 4, 1884

We were both wild over Charleston. It is the most
lovely old city, with about the swellest old houses I
have ever seen this side of the water. The Battery is
almost as pretty as ours must have been.

Both Bess and I were so sorry to miss saying
good-bye to Papa. Bess sends all kind of love to you
and Papa and Dick. We expect to get home Shrove
Tuesday night.

lovingly, Stan

APRIL 23, 1884

DEAR MOMMIE,

We have escaped from the whirlpool of Paris, and are now flying along between Munich and Vienna. We had a very gay time in Paris, although I had to work pretty hard getting Osborne's tapestries. We went to the theatre every night, and Miss Burckhardt, who came over with us, gave us a dinner, and Bessie's uncle gave us several, and has been very kind to us. I liked them all very much.

We went to the Conservatoire one day, and saw some instruments that would set Papa's hair on end. Bess stands the racket pretty well, and is now sound asleep in the carriage.

Munich seemed rather tame after Paris—but still I liked it. The streets are alive with soldiers and bands of music, and you meet officers at every step. We get to Vienna tonight, where we shall stop a few days, and then we are off in earnest for Constantinople, where we arrive Sunday morning. It seems hard to believe.

We are both quite well, as I hope you all are at home, dear mamma. Lots of love to Papa and Dick and thyself.

[Signed with monogram]

NOTE

Charles Clinch, Bessie's uncle, was living in Paris.

Funeral monument, France

TO MRS. PRESCOTT HALL BUTLER

MAY 3, 1884

DEAR NELLY,

I am writing this at the foot of Mount Olympus in Asia, at Brousa, a day's journey from Constantinople. Save that the mountains are higher and the people a little milder, I can see little difference between the continents.

The day before yesterday we made a most heavenly journey. At the head of the Galata Bridge we took a Kaik—a long razor-shaped boat, gorgeous in gilding and decoration—and one in which, by the way, you have to run on an exactly even keel, or you upset; and it was with the utmost difficulty that we balanced the boat, for Bess tipped up both the guide and myself. But this is a digression—imagine us therefore on as soft and lovely a day as the Orient could hold forth, seated in the aforesaid Kaik, with two beturbaned and brawny rowers, and a Dragoman who considered himself Pasha of all the Turkeys— and away we shot into the Bosphorus, past the Old Seraglio, past the Water Gate where the Sultan of Sultans used to flee for his life, and the tower from which he flung his stubborn and bow-strung wives— out onto the Sea of Marmora, and for six miles we flew past Mosques, gardens, palaces and hovels until we reached the Seven Towers—the sea end of the walls of Constantinople. Here three bedecked and

fiery steeds awaited us; and after climbing the towers, and lunching there, we mounted on their backs and cantered along the walls: On one side a great stretch of battlements and towers of all kinds of shapes, piled one against another, and all gone utterly to ruin and covered with the most wonderful verdure—the moat blazing with poppies and wild flowers—and on the other side of the road, a continuous forest of cypresses, with countless graves and tombstones beneath; and over hill and dale, they stretched from the sea to the Golden Horn. We rode up to the Sweet Waters of Europe, and there took a Kaik and rowed back to the place we started from; and I am sure, to our dying day, we will never forget that journey. Please read de Amicis' book I sent Prescott, and make Charles read it. It is utterly hopeless trying to describe Constantinople to you: it is the most beautiful and bewildering of places—the Bazaars alone are enough to set you crazy.

I wisely abstained from buying anything—but having explained to our Dragoman that if I did buy anything I should only buy something very ancient and very cheap, he led me to an out-of-the-way part of the market where they sold things second hand— and I am now the proud possessor of many tiles and thousands of fleas, and am a ruined man. At first I saw little that I wanted; but on pointing out to my guide a mangy old rug on which two greasy Turks

were carding wool, and telling him, (my guide) that that was the sort of thing I wanted, he asked them the price. They grinned, and said 200 piastres—forty francs. I, rather as a joke, offered them twenty, and they took me up quick as a wink; and before you could count twenty, I was surrounded by a great crowd of gesticulating Turks, each offering me the carpet on which he had said his prayers—probably for the last thirty years. I bought seven, much to my guide's horror—and I am sure it will be a long time before that corner of the Bazaar settles down to its usual amount of noise. The day after tomorrow we turn our faces Westward and homewards.

We hardly realize that we are so far away from you all. Bess is the best of girls, and enjoys herself heartily, and I do not think has been over-tired once, save in Paris where we worked all day, and never went to bed before one o'clock. Here we have nothing to do in the evenings, and I have time to bore my friends with letters.

The Clinches were kindness itself to us in Paris, and I became quite fond of them all.

Kiss all the chickadees for me and tell Susie I will answer her beautiful letter with a long one which she might not be able to read.

affly, Stanford

I have shaved off my beard, and Bess says I look like an idiot.

MAY 6, 1884

MY DARLING MAMA,

I just have yours of April 15th. It is too bad that Papa should be bothered so; but it seems to me that a man is bound to get a certain amount of abuse in the world and it is a great mistake to pay any attention to it. We never see the Century or any American paper.

We have been in Asia. Constantinople is the most wonderful place in the world. I meant to write you a long letter about it—but can just squeeze this into the mail. Give my love to Papa, Dick and all. Bess sends love. We are all well and turn our faces westward tomorrow.

Affly, Stan

ATHENS. MAY 18, 1884

DEAR PAPA,

It is the funniest thing in the world, on landing in the Piraeus, to see all the signs in the street in Greek. It is something you never get used to, nor could I, all the time that I was there, at all imagine myself amongst Greeks. As for the language, it might as well be Choctaw. Of course this is caused by my English education; and I had the cheek to ask a rather splendid Greek girl who, by the way spoke Turkish, Armenian, Russian, German, Italian, French—and English quite as well as I did, "Why the Greeks did not talk their language more as the old Greeks did"—and she laughed and said that perhaps the reason why I thought they did not—was because I did not know how to talk old Greek myself.

Modern Athens is an extremely uninteresting city, bright, new, and horribly dusty; and, Shades of Phidias protect us, there is a steam tramway running around the base of the Akropolis—poor Athens! The modern Greeks do not amount to much, but you cannot help sympathizing with them—they have had such hard luck. What little was left them was stolen by the English, and it was only the insurrection which saved the Parthenon and Erectheum from complete restoration at the hands of the Bavarians. It is funny to think, however, that they are still digging up things. I have seen the Treasure of Priam and the Tombs of Agamemnon, and feel quite sot up. Old Homer was not such a liar after all—as some people have tried to make him out to be.

Schliemann is a funny little German with a big head and his house is frescoed with "scenes from the life of Schliemann"—

We took dinner twice with "Little Schuyler" who is Minister to Greece, and to whom I had letters—both he and his wife were very kind.

We are now on the steamer, bound for Sicily, and are both well and happy. Lots of love to all,

affly. Stan

I send you a Greek paper.

Aphrodite, Syracuse

COURTSHIP & MARRIAGE

Chateau in the Loire Valley

Village in France

NAPLES. MAY 31, 1884

MY DARLING MAMA,

I wrote you a long letter—or rather a pooty long let-ter—on the steamer just before we got into Sicily. For some reason or other, I put it in my pocket instead of posting it. Today, in looking over the things there, I found it, and I immediately tore it up—as it consisted chiefly of moralizing on the state of the Turk—and your own moralizing is such silly business, when you happen to read it again.

The Turk simply despises "improvement and progress"—despises, as much as he hates it and the European; and it is an amusing and somewhat sad sight, to see him slowly being pushed to the wall by these very engines. The re-taking of Turkey is being done very silently—but it is none the less sure because it is a peaceful battle.

Sicily is a lovely place, and we enjoyed ourselves thoroughly there. We found it and Athens very hot—but here in Naples the weather is charming, and it is cool. We have been up Vesuvius and to the Blue Grotto, and leave tomorrow for Rome.

Nothing makes an Italian smile as much as the English notion that Rome is more dangerous in June than in winter. It is its most healthy month. I have received yours of the 3rd, your postal card, and yrs. of the 7th of May. Lots of love to all, Bess is well and sends love.

Affly, Stan

ST. MORITZ, ENGADINE. JULY 14, 1884

MY DARLING MOMMIE,

Here we are safe and sound, seven thousand feet in the air in the heart of the Alps. It is not cold!—Oh, no!—and if in an inadvertent moment you take a drink, you have to be taken in and thawed out in front of the kitchen range. The swell rig is fur-lined caps and overcoats; and Bess and I deliberate every morning whether we shall put on three or four undershirts.

Today is our second day here. I shinned up a ten-thousand-foot-high be-glacier-covered alp this morn-ing before breakfast, and skinned all my toes coming down. Here is an edelweiss I picked—not in a snow-bank—the pink flower was, though. I suppose you have all been worrying about the cholera. It is indeed a matter not to be joked about; everybody here is pretty well scared and the unhappy "tourists" plans are likely to be changed at any moment. My sole idea now is to dodge the quarantine. We just escaped sul-phurine fumigation on the Swiss border, and we shall get out of Switzerland by a pass that only nanny-goats use—and so I hope to get the best of the Austrian government. Of course if cholera spreads through France, we shall not go back there. Should it get to England before we do, I do not think it will attack two travellers on the through express between Dover and Liverpool—so do not trouble yourself about us. Bess sends all kind of love—lots to Papa and Dick and to thyself, my darling mother, from thy loving son,

[Signed with caricature]

TO MRS. PRESCOTT HALL BUTLER
MERAN, TYROL
JULY 20, 1884

DEAR NELLY,

I am writing this in Meran, and shall put it in a St. Moritz envelope and post it in Innsbruck—whereby you will have all of the Alps from Milan to the heart of the Tyrol.

We have just escaped out of Switzerland by a pass only chamois and nanny goats use, and so have slipt by the Austrian quarantine and escaped fumigation, or the worse luck of being clapt in a pest house for five days.

We came through in a private post—which is "werry" swell—a Landau and pair, sometimes three horses; and as we wound down the lovely valley of the Adige, our coachmen, decked in the most gorgeous of Tyrolean costumes, would play on their horns to the delight of the quickly assembled villagers. I got your letter in Naples—and as I have had the firm intention of writing you every day since, I must go back there to satisfy my conscience, if for no other reason. But there is another reason. It is a tale—not a horrible one, save in my own imagination—yet it is a tale. I must begin at the beginning. I was ever so much delighted with Madame the Duchess and Monsieur the Duke (della Torre). We put off seeing them until the last days, and were almost sorry that we did so—they were so quiet and simple, and received us so cordially. We took dinner with them, and the wind was high—at least I thought it was—and the linen-beliveried servant made the mistake of leaving the door at one end of the room and the window at the other end—open. The result was awful: as he brought in a macaroni pie, the wind caught the most gorgeous plate-glass butler's pantry door—and with a crash which would have raised the dead, the glass shivered into a thousand pieces. What has this got to do with me? You do not understand!—I was looking at it.

After the storm had cleared off, we took a ride in the King of Naples garden. There is no longer any King of Naples, and he has no garden, still your cousin thinks so, and I must call it so out of compliment to him. We talked about the weather—peacock's tails, and how many young a pheasant could bring forth in a year—and amongst other things, the Duke asked me if I believed in the "evil eye." I intimated that I did not, and that furthermore, in my estimation, anybody who did believe in it was little better than a gibbering idiot. Whereupon both your cousins hastened to inform me that they believed in it—firmly—and then they gave me all manner of conclusive proof: their second son had died, not of natural causes, but because so-and-so had looked at him and admired him; and the Duke gravely informed me that he hated so-and-so with the hate of Hell. Another so-and-so had only gazed at a chandelier and it had fallen to the ground and smashed to atoms, etc., etc., etc.

Now I suppose you will want to know again what this has all got to do with me. My dear Nelly, nothing—yet I had extravagantly praised Giustiniano's beauty, and I remembered how troubled your cousin looked thereat—I had furthermore looked at the butler's pantry door. Of course it is all stuff and nonsense—yet I am so sure that if anything happened to your cousin's family after I left that I would be considered the unhappy cause, that I shall be relieved when I hear that they are all well and happy. We wrote to them but got no answer.

STANFORD WHITE

We were away up in the air in the Engadine, indeed so far up, that it was nothing to shin up a 10,000 ft. be-glacier-covered alp and bring back your sweetheart a bunch of Edelweiss before breakfast. I enclose you a squashed one.

For the last twenty days I have had to use the utmost vigilance to prevent Bess developing a sporadic case of Asiatic Cholera. She persists in liking an affair they call apricot here—which is sometimes ripe, and sometimes greener than a Long Island apple in May. Otherwise we are all well. Everybody is scared out of their lives by the cholera, and definite plans are out of the question. We may have to give up going back to Paris, and Bess will have to return without any Parisian plumage. Love to the child and yourself from your "new" brother.

[Signed with caricature]

LONDON. AUGUST 22, 1884

MY DARLING MOMMIE,

I telegraphed three days ago to my firm, so I suppose they let you know, and you will not be troubled at not hearing from me. We went to Paris in spite of the cholera, and are here, none the worse for going there. I do not know where I got the idea, but I had one—that London was a rather more inexpensive place to stay in than the Continent; but a more outrageously dear place I hope it may never be my misfortune to strike. Neither Bess nor myself could find a decent umbrella for less than six or seven dollars, and every time we go to the theatre, it means two dollars and a half a piece. I doubt if I have enough spondoolica left to fee the porters for taking our luggage off the steamer. We sail as you know on the *Aurania*, on the 30th of August, at 3 p.m. from Liverpool. If all goes well we will be in New York on the following Saturday the 6th of September. When you get this, my darling mother, we shall be far out on the billowy ocean; so here is lots of love to you and Papa and Dick from your affectionate children,

Bess and Stan

P.S. Here is Bess telling me that I have forgotten the most important piece of news, to wit, that you must invest in a pair of spectacles and some gray hairs forthwith our arrival—for I cannot get the idea out of her head that she means to present you with a grandchild before the year is out.

[Signed with caricature]

NOTE

Richard Grant White was born in December 1884 and died of cholera the following August. Lawrence Grant White, White's surviving son, was born in September 1887.

MCKIM, MEAD & WHITE, NEW YORK
OCTOBER 6, 1903

DEAR LARRIE,

You are a nice boy, to go away without letting me know about your birthday when I asked you to. I am getting old and getting a very POOR memory, and you are young and have no excuse; so I want you to write me always four or five days beforehand to remind me of your birthday. This little electric thing is not much of a present, but still may amuse you, and you can hang it up, alongside of your bed without setting it afire.

Your mother said that you had very hazy ideas about your allowance, and didn't know how long the amount you now have to your credit was for. Now Larrie I told you very carefully and distinctly that you would get $60 a month to cover all your expenses and disbursements at the school and away from it, and that there would be deposited to your credit $180 every three months. For this last three months (that is from the 1st of October until the 1st of January) I have given you $200 instead of $180, but the $20 must always stay in the bank. That is, when you drew your account down to this $20 you must stop, and it must always remain there. You are to balance your account in your checkbook with each check you draw, stating exactly what each check is drawn for. When, however, you draw your check for cash or pocket money, you must keep an account of how you spend this in a little petty cash book which you can keep. In this way, and in this way only, can you see how you are spending your money, and how to make it last as long as possible. The one thing you want to absolutely set your mind against is ever

thinking of spending more money than you have; and in fact the only way to do is to arrange your expenses in such a way that you have a little reserve, and to get into this habit, as it is only by this means that you will have an easy time through life.

Be good

affly, your Paw

OCTOBER 13, 1903

DEAR GUS

We are to have another portrait show for the benefit of the Orthopaedic Hospital for crippled children. We would like to have any one of your portrait reliefs that you can send, that is, Stevenson's, Howells and his daughter, or any new ones that you have done. We of course assume all responsibility as to insurance, expenses, etc.

Affy, Stanford

MARCH 18, 1904

MY DEAR GUS:

You long-nosed farmer you! What do you mean by backing out of The Brook? It is not your "mun" that we want but your name and yourself. That is, we want you as a nest egg and an attraction for a dozen men whom we want in, and I think in the end will come in. What we want to make of the Club is one that is not all society men, like the Knickerbocker, or men of the world, like the Union and Metropolitan, or a Lunch Club, like The Players, or one where mainly actors congregate, like The Lambs, or a Sleepy Hollow, like The Century; but a very quiet, small Club, something like the Beefsteak Club in London, where you will have the freedom of some of

Miniature of Lawrence Grant White, probably painted by Ellen Emmet Rand, c. 1904.

the Clubs I have mentioned and the quietness of others, and where you will always be sure, from lunch time to two or three in the morning, to find three or four men you will always be glad to see and no one that you will not be glad to see.

I think that, once the Club is started, and you have tried it for a year, you will want to stay in it; and I think that McKim and a lot of fellows that you know and like, in addition to those that are already in, will also join it. But it will really break my heart if you don't join and at least make the trial.

Lovingly, Stanford

RISTIGOUCHE CLUB. JUNE 1904

MY DARLING BESS,

I have your second letter. What I worry about Larrie is not paying the thousand dollars, but getting an Autocar when the experts I trust in all say a Franklin is ever so much better. Larrie has been persuaded into this by the agent, evidently, nor does he know whether he would not like a Franklin better—or how Autocars wear; every car seems good when it is new. If he can get out of it he should, and leave the final settlement until I get back. If he cannot, why let me know—and I will manage to pay the $1000.

I have sworn off everything but one drink of whiskey before dinner; but Jim [Breese] says it is big enough to kill an ox. I exercise regularly—much to Jim's amusement when he found out it was to reduce my stummick. He says the flapjacks I eat every day would put a pussy's stomach on anyone; in fact he thinks the enclosed pictures exactly fill the bill as far as I go.

I hope you will have enough salmon by the time you get this—which should be the morning of Susie's wedding. Give my love to them all and say I am sorry I am not to be there.

lovingly, Stanford

NOTE

Larry White eventually did get a car by meeting his father's challenge that he dismantle an engine and then restore it to working order.

James Lawrence Breese, real estate investor and amateur photographer, for whom White designed The Orchard in Southampton, Long Island.

SEPTEMBER 23, 1904

DEAR GUSTIBUS:

I have been making many different studies for the
scheme of steps and columns for your new Lincoln;
but, as usual, the simple scheme is much the best. The
whole thing in fact resolves itself into the proper pro-
portions of the circle and the columns to your figure
and to the surroundings; and I think the final studies
which I now send you are about as good as I can do.
Of course, I do not know how much the Committee
have in hand, or are willing to stand, and I really do
not know how much this plan will cost. I send it to
you, and, if you approve, I will get estimates at once
and then we will be able to shave them down if it is
found to be necessary.

Affy, Stanford

MCKIM, MEAD & WHITE
160 FIFTH AVENUE
FEBRUARY 7, 1905

MY DARLING BESS,

I got your second cable saying "All serene," from
Taormina, and sent return cables both to Taormina
and care of Turner & Co. I went south, as you know,
on the Friday after you left, stopping at Washington,
getting to Thomasville on Sunday afternoon. I had
caught cold, and while I was in Thomasville I had a
regular old-fashioned earache. I got well of it and left
for Ormond the next day; but it has left me really
quite deaf, and I am going to Dr. Sharp every morning to get back to where I was before. But even this,
the doctor seems to think, will take some weeks.

When I got to Ormond, in Florida, I found it
colder really than I have ever experienced in my life.

Of course I did not know it then, but a frightful
blizzard had struck the whole country: the wind was
blowing twenty-five miles an hour down there, with
the thermometer down to twenty-two, and it afterward went down to eighteen; and it seemed as cold as
forty below zero up in New York. Everybody froze to
death except Jimmie Breese, who had his great big
polar bear overcoat and all his winter paraphernalia.

The races were not very amusing, and if it had not
been for Mrs. R.R. Thomas, whom I was with most
of the time, I should have come home two days earlier
than I did. I went ten miles in nine minutes and thir-
teen seconds, however, in Wallace's racer. It was as
near flying, I think, as I will ever come to, and that
experience was worth going a long way for.

Since I have been back it seems to me I have been
doing nothing but go to dinners, and I have made up
my mind to answer all of them now that "expected
absence from town" will prevent my coming. The
Hyde ball was the most gorgeous affair I ever saw. The
costumes, generally, were nowhere near as pretty or as
elaborate as at Bradley Martin's but the whole thing
was splendidly done—the servants were all in gorgeous livery, and there were guards with drawn
swords, and spears, and 'niggers' in Eastern costumes,
and all sorts of things. The supper room was an
absolute bower, and was really the prettiest thing I
have ever seen in my life. Some of the girls looked
beautifully, especially Mrs. Widener, and, as to Mrs.
MacKay, she went as Theodora, in a gown of spun silver and gold all encrusted with turquoise, and with a
great turquoise and silver crown on her head, the
whole effect being that of silver and blue. As far as I
could make out, she had absolutely nothing but her

dress on. Her train was at least ten feet long and was carried by two little bare-armed and bare-legged negroes with gorgeous gold dresses. I send you a caricature, in the "World," in which your very 'umble is up in the right-hand corner.

Larrie is very well indeed: he came on just before the Hyde ball, and is here now. All the time he was here before I only dined with him once, with mother, at the Dudleys as he was engaged every other time. Everybody is all very well, and everything is getting along nicely. I do not feel as if I had all the comforts of home up at Charlie's, and swear and damn now and then; and every now and then accept two invitations for one evening: otherwise, as I am working hard, I have not much time to pine and be lonely.

Larrie and Otto, by the way, the last time he was here, distinguished themselves by getting arrested for speeding. The bicycle policeman chased them for five blocks and finally caught them at 59th and Fifth Avenue. Larrie could not find me and went to the Dudleys and borrowed $100 from them and mother to bail Otto out, and I sent him back to college Sunday night, and then had to appear at the Yorkville Police Court. Braman went with me, however, and fixed the thing up with the Judge, and Otto was left off and everything was serene.

I am getting along pretty well at Charlie McKim's, although I do not see much of him, and I have a pretty hard time with the wild Irish girls, as they have not caught on to my ways yet—and it is not like home at all at all, and I wish you were here many a time; but do not, now that you are over there, think of coming back before May. Go to Ireland and then go back to Paris and enjoy yourself.

Larrie will get along all right, and it is a great deal better, now that you are over there, not to hurry. But take it easy. All well at St. James, and everybody well and everything serene here. Incidentally however I have not yet got a letter from you. With many kisses and hugs

lovingly, Stan

NOTE

While Bessie was in Europe, White had sublet the Gramercy Park house and was staying with McKim in order to reduce his mounting debts.

The Bradley Martin Ball, held in February 1897, epitomized the excesses of the Gilded Age. The Grand Ballroom of the Waldorf-Astoria was transformed into the Hall of Mirrors at Versailles for the evening, and the negative publicity that ensued forced the Martins to take up residence in England.

James Hazen Hyde, an heir to the Equitable Life Assurance Company, was the host of a lavish costume ball held at Sherry's on January 31, 1905. Many of White's clients attended, including Mrs. Stuyvesant Fish for whom he had designed a house at 78th Street and Madison Avenue in 1900 and Mrs. Clarence MacKay for whom he built Harbor Hill in Roslyn, New York, 1899–1902.

FEBRUARY 17, 1905

MY DARLING BESS,

I have just got your letter from Palermo and cable from Rome. I sent you a cable every week and have written three times a week, so far, and am glad you are having so good a time. I have been having a pretty tough one. Long before you receive this I suppose you will have seen in the Paris edition of the New York Herald an account of the fire which destroyed the storage warehouse. I purposely kept away from reporters, so that the accounts in the newspaper were very meagre, and I send you one which is at hand. Many of the insurances had run out, but the most unfortunate circumstance is that the things I took from the house, as I expected they would be only there for a few weeks, I neglected to transfer the insurance on. The floors fell in, and sheets of water were poured over everything, which froze in a solid mass, and it will be quite a while before they unearth the debris and I find out exactly what is saved or lost. This misfortune is certainly a hard blow after all the others, but after all there are so many, many worse things that could have happened that I suppose I should not be too "disheartened," so I am grinning and going back to work as hard as I can. Do not worry dearest.

Stanford

FEBRUARY 24, 1905

MY DARLING BESS,

I have today received your letter written on your return from Naples. I answered today in care of McKay Hooker, Rome, as I supposed that would get to you quickest. All my cables from now on, however, I will send care of Hoddinger & Co., Paris.

Larrie and mother and everything all right. The fire is turning out worse than I expected, but, at the same time, it is impossible even, as yet, to form any idea exactly what has happened. The floors fell in, and some of the walls on top of them, and then tons and tons of water were poured over the debris, and this froze in a solid mass. Until the ice is removed, and the bricks and beams taken up, it is impossible to know exactly what is saved. Some of the things have come out almost whole, and many things are a total loss. Whatever damage has been done, however, is irreparable, and the only thing to do is to pluck up spirit and bear it. As Charlie McKim said, so many worse things could have happened that the best way is to thank Heaven that this calamity, and not any of the others, took place. It is too bad that this should come while you are trying to have a good time, but I hope that you will cheer up and enjoy yourself. The sale—or rather, the sale of those things which are left, has been postponed until the 23rd of April. I have put fifty dollars to the credit of your account at the 2nd National Bank and shall send you a thousand francs to get a dress in Paris. Do have a good time and enjoy yourself.

lovingly, Stanford

McKIM, MEAD & WHITE,
160 FIFTH AVENUE,
NEW YORK.

February 24, 1905.

My darling Bess

I have today received your letter written on your return from Naples. I answered today in care of McKay Hooker, Rome, as I supposed that would get to you quickest. All my cables from now on, however, I will send care of Hoddinger & Co., Paris.

Larrie and mother and everything all right. The fire is turning out worse than I expected, but, at the same time, it is impossible even, as yet, to form any idea exactly what has happened. The floors fell in, and some of the walls on top of them, and then tons and tons of water were poured over the debris, and this froze in a solid mass. Until the ice is removed, and the bricks and beams taken up, it is impossible to know exactly what is saved. Some of the things have come out almost whole, and many things are a total loss. Whatever damage has been done, however, is irreparable, and and the only thing to do is to pluck up spirit and bear it. As Charlie (McKim) said, so many worse things could have happened that the best way is to thank Heaven that this calamity, and not any of the others, took place. but It is too bad that this should come while you are trying to have a good time, but I hope that you will cheer up and enjoy yourself. The "sale -

To his wife, February 24, 1905

OCTOBER 25, 1905

DEAR GUSTY:

When I was in Syracuse years ago, I was perfectly ravished by a Greek Venus which they have there. I made a lot of drawings of her myself, which I was very proud of, and am still; but I never could find a photograph of her, and I have always regretted that I did not have one made. Lo and behold, however, in the Sunday Herald of October 8th they have a photograph of her, and I send it up to you and want to know if you do not think she is the 'most beautifullest' thing that ever was in this world.

Also, when I was in Paris, I saw, in a little antiquity place, in the backyard, some workmen from the Louvre setting up what seemed to me a wonderful statue which had just been dug up and had come, by underground passage, from Greece. I had a photograph sent me, and I include it. It is life size, of Paros marble, and of the most beautiful color you ever saw, and can be bought for fifteen thousand dollars. It is of course late work, but it does seem to me as if I ought to get somebody to 'nab' it. Please send the photograph back to me and let me know what you think of it.

Affy, Stan

NEW YORK. MARCH 17, 1906

DEAR GUS:

I send you with this a careful drawing for the Phillips Brooks Monument. In your letter to me you ask that I should send drawings for both the square and the circular one, but I am so positive that the square form is infinitely the best, everyone agreeing with me, McKim, Kendall and Phil Richardson, that I beg you to give up the idea of the round one and go ahead with the square one. The round one might look well from the front, but all the other views would be complicated and ugly.

Affy, Stanford

MAY 11, 1906

BELOVED!!

Why do you explode so at the idea of Charlie and myself coming up to Windsor? If you think our desire came from any wish to see any damned fine spring or fine roads you are not only mistaken, but one of the most modest and unassuming men with so 'beetly' a brow and so large a nose 'wot is.' We were coming up to bow down before the sage and seer we admire and venerate. So weather be damned, and roads, too!

Of course, when it comes to a question of Charlie and myself doing anything, large grains of salt have got to be shaken all over the 'puddin.' I am a pretty hard bird to snare; and, as for Charlie, he varies ten thousand times more than a compass does from the magnetic pole; so all this may end in smoke; but the cherry blossoms are out, and to hell with the Pope!"

[Signed with caricature]

Stanford White, photographed by Gertrude Kasebier, c. 1905.

FURTHER READING

Andrews, Wayne. *Architecture, Ambition, & Americans: A Social History of American Architecture.* New York, 1964.

Baker, Paul R. *Stanny: The Gilded Life of Stanford White.* New York: The Free Press, 1989.

Baldwin, Charles C. *Stanford White.* New York: Dodd, Mead, 1931. Reissued in paperback with an introduction by Paul Goldberger by Da Capo Press, New York, 1976.

Dryfhout, John H. *The Work of Augustus Saint-Gaudens.* Hanover and London: University Press of New England, 1982.

Lowe, David Garrard. *Stanford White's New York.* New York: Doubleday, 1992.

McKim, Mead & White. *A Monograph of the Work of McKim, Mead & White 1879-1915.* 4 vols. New York Architectural Book Publishing Co., 1915. Reissued in one volume, 1973.

Mumford, Lewis. *The Brown Decades.* New York: Dover Publications, 1955.

Roth, Leland. *McKim, Mead & White, Architects.* New York: Harper & Row, 1983.

Saint-Gaudens, Augustus. *The Reminiscences of Augustus Saint-Gaudens.* Edited by Homer Saint-Gaudens. 2 vols. London: Andrew Melrose, 1913.

White, Lawrence Grant. *Sketches and Designs of Stanford White.* New York: The Architectural Book Publishing Co., 1920.

Wilson, Richard Guy. *McKim, Mead & White, Architects.* New York: Rizzoli International Publications, 1983.